PRINTING FOR PLEASURE

PRINTING
FOR PLEASURE

JOHN RYDER

HENRY REGNERY COMPANY
CHICAGO

To my Wife
and to my Publisher

© John Ryder 1955
New material Copyright © John Ryder 1976
Revised edition published in
Great Britain in 1976 by
The Bodley Head Ltd., London
and in the United States in 1977 by
Henry Regnery Company
180 North Michigan Avenue
Chicago, Illinois 60601
Printed in Great Britain
ISBN 0-8092-7810-3

Foreword

You may notice that this book first appeared in 1955. I wish it had appeared thirty years earlier, when, like many other schoolboys, I was tempted and then caught by those famous Adana advertisements published so regularly in the back pages of *The Magnet* – or was it *The Boy's Own Paper*? – offering me the power to print anything 'from a chemist's label to an illustrated magazine'. An illustrated magazine! What vistas that opened up in front of me, what emancipation from the jellygraph and the John Bull outfit. But alas, reality was sobering. Printing is an intricate subject. The basic facts that with years of hindsight now seem so obvious I found exceedingly difficult to pin down. What exactly was a *fount* of type? Why were some letters called Old Style and other, spikier-looking ones, called Modern? Why weren't they all the same? And *furniture* . . . heavens, what was I letting myself in for? As for the niceties of typography, or its history, neither the school library nor the local bookshop had anything to offer me. *Printing Explained*, by Herbert Simon and Harry Carter, was not published until 1931. From then on, as the list of books and periodicals included in this book will show, the information one needed gradually became more accessible.

John Ryder would have soon put me on the rails. His book is compact, brief, and deals with essentials. By essentials I mean not only the techniques of printing, assembling the type and transferring ink from type to paper. If you are a beginner, it is just as essential to have some knowledge of the art of typography, and you will find it set down here with enviable concision. The right use of space, of course, only comes with experience, with the training of the eye; but at least this book will make you aware that such a skill needs to be acquired if really satisfying work is to be done.

It would be superfluous to repeat advice already given so clearly in the pages that follow. But it is perhaps worth emphasising to the beginner that this book is about printing for pleasure. Once you are equipped with a press, however humble, and a case or two of type, the temptation to print for profit is very great. Pleasure and profit can indeed be reconciled, but if you wish to explore to the full the possibilities for experiment suggested here, and your time is limited, you will be wise not to saddle yourself with the orders of importunate friends. Printing five hundred letterheads on a table platen is not the most agreeable of pastimes.

Instead, therefore, I would urge you to ponder chapter six, 'Developing a Taste for Experiment', where, as the author rightly says, 'it is a pity that few private presses have concerned themselves with experimental techniques since it is here on the amateur's workbench (a place from which the time-sheet and the wage-bill are absent), that experiments can be made and repeated without end and without fear of bankruptcy'.

And so be guided by Ryder. He will not let you down.

Vivian Ridler

November 1975

CONTENTS

Editor's Note

Twenty years separate the first and the present editions of this book which now, in quite a large part, may claim to be a new work.

My special thanks to Heather Copley and Christopher Chamberlain who drew the illustrations on pages 21, 27, 28, 33, 42, 59, 60, 61, 62, 63, 64, and 84; to Iain Bain, Canterbury College of Art, David Gentleman, Kenneth Hardacre, John Petts, Lotte Reiniger, Robert Wyss and Joseph Low for permission to show illustrations; to Michael Harvey for his demonstration of lettering design; to Sem Hartz, Susan Shaw, Giovanni Mardersteig, Mike Parker, F. E. Pardoe and Willis Tompkins for permission to include examples from the *Miniature Folio of Private Presses*.

Invaluable help in the locating of sources of equipment has been given by William Reuter, John Lehman, A. G. Bagnall, and, in general, by David Chambers, James Moran and Kim Taylor.

The reader's attention is called to the glossary of printing terms in common use which starts on page 121. Many of these terms naturally occur in the text of this book and the first time they are used are printed in *italics*.

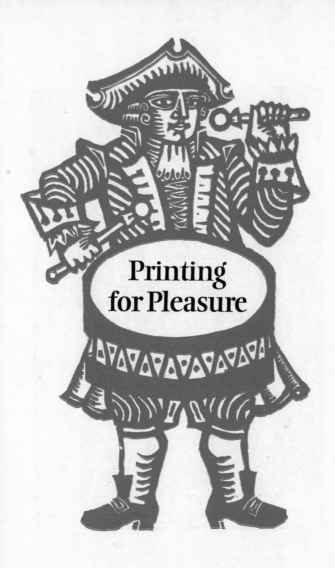

Printing
for Pleasure

This cut, made by a student at the Canterbury College of Art in 1954, was originally used for a college announcement.

Prelum
Ascēsianū.

I.S.

*Sixteenth-century press shown on one of the devices of the
printer Ascensius of Lyons.*

[1]

Introduction:
Pleasure as Profit

In this small book I can do no more than introduce my subject and hope that its theme – pleasure as a natural result of the process of printing – will gain your interest and sympathy.

For many years of my life printing and pleasure have been inseparably linked. I do not find this surprising since the process of printing is itself fascinating and the results obtainable even from meagre equipment can be really good. What you choose to print and the way in which you print it are largely responsible for the amount of pleasure to be gained but I would not deny that printing can be absolute drudgery.

Moreover it is not only the kind of printing but also the attitude of the printer which determines whether this activity shall be profit-making drudgery or a pleasurable pastime. You should dispense with any idea of running a small press as a money-making side-line. In the first place to do so would put you under obligation to people who perhaps know nothing about print. You may be asked to produce items with which you have little or no sympathy and become involved in the keeping of accounts. It would be far better to use your equipment as an instrument of design, to give your designs freely and to take friendship in return. If

THOMAS BEWICK'S

MORBID, RIBALD AND SCATOLOGICAL

HUMOURS

here displayed in nine of his
tail-pieces printed from the

ORIGINAL BLOCKS

IAIN BAIN AT
THE LAVEROCK PRESS
MCMLXXII

*Title-page made by the Bewick collector and scholar
at his own press.*

your growing circle of friends does not quickly convince you of the value of this attitude you may be sure you are mis-spending your leisure and that your talent lies elsewhere.

Printing will be most creative if the press and the materials are handled with that end in view. For instance at the start it may be amusing to set up an essay, story or poem of some length but, before long, the task of *composing* line after line and *page* after page of type is likely to become irksome. Whereas if you choose to print typographical ephemera and to experiment with various *settings* of the same few words and ornaments you will teach yourself a great deal about design and at the same time enjoy the very rewarding pleasure of creating a style – or at least adapting a style to your needs. The discovery that a few words on, say, an invitation card can be re-arranged in a dozen entirely different ways will open your eyes to the problems involved in planning print. Then, when the type is set in such a way as to suit your own message and your own emphasis on the parts of that message, questions relating to paper (surface texture, thickness, colour, size and shape), to the colour of ink and to decoration arise and have to be settled. I say 'have to be settled', but really these questions only have to be settled if you are determined to fulfil a creative urge. Once you begin to examine all kinds of printed matter you will find that a very great deal of it has escaped any serious thought with regard to design and presentation. The important questions have been answered inadequately if at all.

This is where you, equipped with a handful of well-chosen types, may be able to find solutions to many everyday problems. You have only to collect commer-

Rutt's press poses the problem: Pleasure or drudgery?

cial letter-headings or compliments slips or typographical greetings cards or invitations and announcements to realize that the majority of these ephemeral items have been produced without much thought. Although at first it may be easier to criticize than to improve, the knowledge and the skill required to criticize constructively will come with practice.

There is no mystery or magic in printing or in designing print. The few short chapters of this book will tell you briefly how it is done, where to look for good examples, what kind of press and what *founts* of type to choose. Where the equipment may be bought is set out in Chapter 9. A glance at some of the unorthodox techniques described in Chapter 6 will dispel any idea that a simple press is limited in its scope and should your enthusiasm make you ambitious there is no doubt that small presses are capable of creating quite a stir.

It would be well to examine your temperament before seriously committing yourself to either an apprentice or a partner. Both these forms of assistance imply an unusual amount of understanding and of give-and-take. An article by R. H. Slaney in the columns of *The Observer* in the early 1950s suggested that young poets should set up and share the expenses of a press for the printing of their own work. This is an excellent idea in theory but in practice it is extremely unlikely that two or more poets could amicably share equipment of this nature. If possible do without assistance, financial or otherwise, and retain complete control over materials, style and output.

Perhaps I ought to qualify my earlier suggestion that it is drudgery to set pages of type. The slow business of building up words and lines and pages can become tiresome but on the other hand the very fact of knowing exactly where you are going and that the going is steady and long-lasting may very well appeal. Here is something absorbing, creative, perhaps soothing, that will occupy hand and mind for a long time. Growth of the work will be slow but the finished product, provided that a text worthy of the labour has been chosen, may well be rewarding. Personally I look on this form of pleasure a little sceptically – possibly because design and experiment appeal more strongly to me. Setting whole pages of type, or printing more than fifty copies of anything, belong, as far as I am concerned, to the composing-machine and the power-press. The thought of performing such tasks entirely by hand puts me in mind of Rutt's press from Hansard's *Typographia* where the poor man turning the handle is undoubtedly something of a drudge.

Before you consider taking up printing as a pastime there is a very important question to be answered. It relates to a characteristic of printing practice, namely, orderliness. Without this personal quality printing cannot be carried out successfully. Once it is understood that, even to begin with, you will be using somewhere between 800 and 1,000 different characters, you will realize the necessity of keeping your material in order. If you do not 'mind your p's and q's' throughout this range of characters, confusion will bring your enterprise to a standstill. Keeping order is a simple procedure only if you recognize that it is essential. It is because this sense of order may be lacking in, or be abhorrent to, some people that I issue the warning. There is no physical difficulty about keeping types in order since printing equipment is made specially to facilitate it. However, if orderliness runs counter to your temperament then beware of printing types.

Finally I must add that, although you can begin with very little equipment, it is most important to choose well. Especially the choice of the type needs care. When I began to print I chose an unsuitable *face* but perhaps I should say, in fairness to myself, I had at that time no idea how to obtain good types. In my ignorance I chose a face that, on closer acquaintance, I found impossible to live with.

[2]
A Small Press for
the Miniature Workshop

Before you decide what printing press to buy there are some considerations to be taken into account. For instance, how much space can be allocated to the new venture? What are the conditions of this proposed space? Unless you have plenty of room and a good solid floor it would be unwise to think of installing a press as large and as heavy as, say, an Albion, Columbian or treadle *platen*. Also what quality and kind of work do you wish to produce? For taking a few *impressions* of *blocks* or a line or two of type a small office copying press may well prove adequate, but should you need to print a hundred impressions or more of greetings- or invitation-cards then a small vertical platen press would be much more useful. If on the other hand you want to print quite large pages or *broadsheets* something like an Albion or a Washington press will be needed, and a moderately large setting can also be printed on the Adana quarto horizontal platen press. This latter machine can be used for hand-inking like the Albions, or for automatic inking like the small vertical platens. It will take a single sheet of paper measuring 203 × 254 mm and, when using the press for hand-inking, it is possible to let the paper overhang the side edges. Thus the 254 mm limit remains but your paper could be 254 × 609 mm and in three separate printings all of this area could be printed on.

However, don't be tempted to spend a lot of money on a good platen press just because it is capable of printing quickly, say, up to 800 impressions an hour. You may be being influenced in the wrong direction. The temptation to 'make it pay for itself' will be strong and if you yield to this temptation the press will make you its slave and will only employ you as its motor and minder. As I see it there could be no possible pleasure in this and the whole aspect of printing becomes in danger of being switched from pleasure to mercenary profit. Yet this is by no means the whole picture. There is pleasure to be had from the actual process of printing, from the skill of setting and printing a page of type; a number of famous books have been printed in this way – a page at a time on a small platen handpress. Provided that you are entirely free to choose what shall be printed and the way in which it shall be printed, the greatest dangers will be past, but even so, you will be making yourself a slave to some extent. The hours of toil will certainly be disproportionate to the hours of pleasure, for once you have started, say, a sixteen-page booklet you must go on to the end, however many months it takes, otherwise the whole effort will have been wasted. I would certainly deprecate spending leisure hours at the handle of a machine.

To sum up, the size and weight of the press, the speed at which it will print and the size of paper on which it will print, are the main considerations before buying. You must also find out about the availability of presses. Columbian, Albion and Washington presses are antiques and you will be dependent on finding an

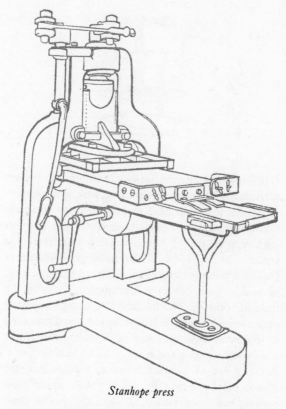

Stanhope press

old one. Sometimes, by reading or advertising in printing trades magazines, secondhand machines of various
kinds may be obtained at bargain prices. Re-built platen
presses can often be purchased from their makers at
substantially reduced rates. There are also printers'
suppliers who re-condition Albion and Columbian
presses, and the Adana presses are readily available
(see Chapter 9).

Standing-screw press

Before examining the various hand-printing presses individually let us take a very brief look at the history of presses from the time of Gutenberg to the early nineteenth century. From the middle of the fifteenth century to the end of the eighteenth century there was virtually no development. Thomas Bewick's *History of Quadrupeds* was printed in 1790 on much the same kind of wooden press as were Gutenberg's *Bibles* in the fifteenth century. No fundamental change occurred until 1800 when Earl Stanhope invented and produced an iron press. George Clymer of Philadelphia invented, and brought to England in 1817, his Columbian press. R. W. Cope of London began to manufacture the Albion press and by 1862 no less than 4,300 of these presses had been made. In 1822 the Acorn press appeared in America and was the forerunner of R. Hoe and Company's Washington press produced about 1827. These presses, though they have not been manufactured for many years, remain in use today.

It is interesting to note that William Nicholson made drawings for, and patented, a cylinder press in 1790 and that, so it appears, the invention never developed beyond a handful of drawings and a patent. Then, in

1810, a German engineer, temporarily resident in London, constructed an iron press on traditional lines but driven by steam. One year later this inventor, Friedrich Koenig, patented the first power-driven cylinder press and in 1814 *The Times* was printed on Koenig's steam cylinder presses.

The simplest form of handpress is a standing-screw press, usually described as an office copying press or nipping press. You might find one in a junk shop.

You can see from the illustration that it is hardly a printing press but it would serve adequately for proofing small blocks or some lines of type tied-up or secured

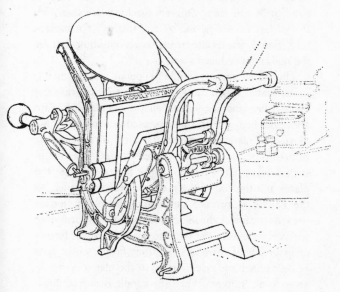

'Model' hand platen press

in a *chase*. I have seen a nicely printed Christmas card (a wood block and the word 'greetings' set in type) done on this kind of press, and a second colour had been added by hand. The *bed* of such a press measures about 254 × 305 mm. One such press was converted by David Chambers (Cuckoo Hill Press) into an efficient printing machine complete with *tympan* and *frisket* and a bed sliding along rails under the platen.

The next machine to be considered is the hand platen press. This is of quite complicated structure based on the commercial platen printing press and adapted for hand operation. It will print quickly and, with skill in adjustment, can be made to print as well as any small press. It is the most popular design of hand press and many different machines are available. Prices vary according to size and quality of manufacture. Some presses are available re-conditioned from the makers at reduced rates.

The platen press is simple to operate and the inking is automatic. When the *forme* has been locked into the vertical bed and ink spread on the circular ink plate above the bed, the handle is pressed downwards. This moves the platen (on which the sheet of paper to be printed is placed) towards the bed by a *toggle* action in such a way that when the paper meets the type the platen and the bed of the press are exactly parallel. As the handle is pressed down and the platen moves towards the forme the inking rollers come upwards over the type and onto the circular ink plate. Steel fingers (grippers) hold the sheet of paper firmly whilst it is being printed and release it when the platen is moved away from the type. When the handle is moved down the paper comes into contact with the type and an im-

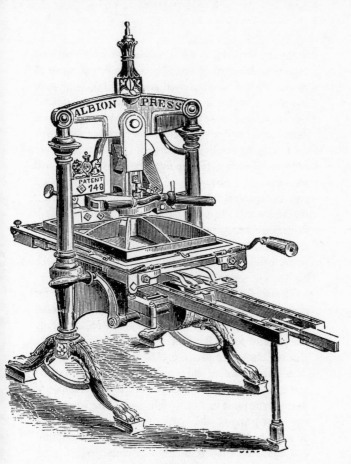

Albion press

pression is made. Let the handle come up again, the type is re-inked, and the printed sheet may be removed. The machine illustrated on page 21 is Excelsior's Model hand platen. In this kind of press the sheet of paper to be printed can be larger than the platen. In fact it can overhang on the three unhinged sides without becoming damaged or inked. It is therefore possible to print a sheet containing eight pages of a book one page at a time – each page as big as the chase of the press will allow. In this way the sheet printed both sides and folded twice will give an eight-page section of a book for sewing or stapling into covers. The exact position of print on each page (the *imposition* of the sheet) will require careful planning and, unless you have enough type to set all eight pages before commencing to print, the sequence of the folded pages will have to be followed. Print page 1 first, then page 2 on the other side of the sheet backing page 1 and so on. The sheet, when folded twice, will give a sequence of eight pages and only the top edge of the folded sheet need be cut.

The small platen press is really more suitable for printing letter-headings, greetings cards, *bookplates* and labels and for any small job which requires only one printing for each colour. Also it is necessary to note that the chase of a platen press fits into a vertical bed. The importance of this will be clear after looking through Chapter 4 because the correct technique of setting type must be strictly followed. Otherwise, when you start printing, the type will fall out of the chase. In a flat-bed press, where the bed is horizontal, simplified methods of typesetting can be employed.

If you have room enough for a large press it might be worth enquiring about a treadle machine. A second-hand treadle platen in good condition can sometimes be found for a reasonably modest sum.

The next presses to consider are the Albion, the Columbian, and the Washington. Of these the Albion is the most common in Britain and the Washington

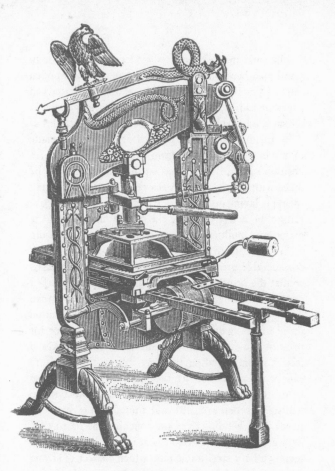

Columbian press

the most common in America. Albion presses have been made in several sizes the smallest of which is named 'Foolscap folio'. This name gives the size of the platen and the largest sheet it will print is Crown folio or 254×381 mm.

The smaller presses have short legs and are made to stand on a bench or on a specially constructed wooden frame. The larger presses, like those illustrated on pages 23 and 25, stand on the floor. All are operated in the same way, which may briefly be described as follows:

By turning the handle the bed of the press is made to travel along runners from under the platen to a position clear of the platen so that the type may be inked with a hand-roller. A *proof* can be taken by inking the type, laying on a sheet of paper, closing the tympan, rolling the bed (by turning the handle) underneath the platen and pulling the lever which, by toggle action, moves the platen downwards towards the type with considerable pressure. This procedure is now reversed so that the printed sheet can be taken off the type. For accurate printing, *press-points* are fixed on the tympan which pierce the sheet and so enable the exact position to be found again for printing a second colour or for printing the other side of the sheet (*backing-up*). Also a frisket is employed so that any ink on the furniture cannot be picked up by the paper. The frisket also holds the clean sheet of paper close to the tympan whilst it is being closed and therefore prevents the paper from bending over and touching the inked type before the correct position is reached. The frisket is merely a light steel frame onto which a cover of strong paper is attached and then cut so that once the frisket and tympan are closed only the areas of type to be printed are accessible to the clean sheet of paper. A proficient printer will make something like 100 impressions an hour.

This brief description will give you a rough idea of how printing is done with an Albion press. For a more

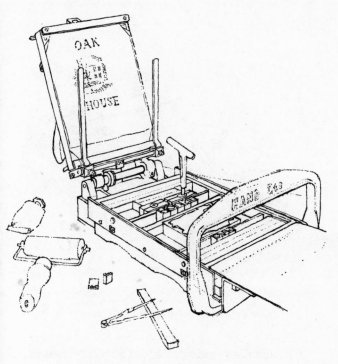

Adana quarto horizontal platen press

detailed account you should read Simon and Carter's
Printing Explained (1931).

Finally we come to the machine most frequently dis-
cussed in this book – the Adana quarto press. I chose
this press for my own workshop because it does not
need to be secured to the bench or table on which it
is worked. It is a small, light, simple form of machine
with a horizontal bed measuring 254×203 mm. It is
ideally suited to the designer who may wish to take a
few impressions of many different arrangements of

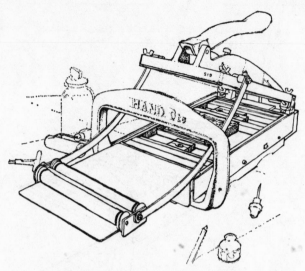

Adana quarto horizontal platen press – using rollers

type. For this purpose a simplified form of typesetting can be employed.

The drawing above shows the automatic inking system. The two rollers are attached by curved arms to the sides of the platen. As the press is opened and shut the rollers travel over the ink-plate, across the type, and then back over the type again and on to the ink-plate. The printer holds the handle in one hand and lays-on and takes-off paper with the other in much the same way as for a hand platen press, but with a some-what reduced speed. A pressure adjustment screw bearing on the underside of the handle enables the correct pressure to be given when printing anything from a single character to a complete forme of type.

The drawing on page 27 shows the press as it is used for hand inking. When the rollers, together with the two arms, have been removed, the press becomes a simple instrument. To the designer of print it is little more of a machine than a pen is to a calligrapher, and, in my opinion, just as essential. Further, although the Albion may be equal to this press in most respects and has a better and more powerful action (lever and toggle) to take the impression, the smallest Albion requires more space, cannot be carried about like this Adana, and is sometimes difficult to find at any price.

In America several small presses are available. The platen presses are similar to the English makes. The Washington is an American equivalent of the Albion.

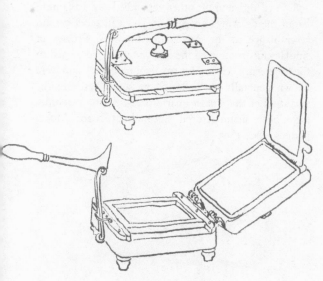

Parlour press, 1846

For many years, in both England and America, hand-presses have been specially made for private printing. As far back as 1846 Edward Cowper (the printing engineer who, together with Augustus Applegath, produced newspaper printing presses for *The Times*) invented a *flatbed* platen for the use of amateurs. This

'Parlour' press, as it was called, was manufactured by Holtzapffel in two sizes, one with a bed measuring 178 × 153 mm, and the other with a bed 381 × 254 mm. From the drawings on page 29 you will see a certain resemblance to the Adana quarto press. Presses of similar construction to the Parlour press were used in the nineteenth century for small jobbing work and were known generally as 'bellows' presses. These are the ancestors of the Adana quarto press. Adana machines have been manufactured since about 1920; Model platens since 1865.

Engravings by David Gentleman for the Lion and Unicorn Press book Births, Marriages and Deaths, *privately issued in 1954*

[3]
Choose a Face
You Can Live With

Choosing your first typeface to experiment with is an important step in the setting up of a small press. Many private printers have designed or commissioned their own types but, on the assumption that you will not be doing this, you must consult the founders' and suppliers' catalogues and make your choice from these sources (see Chapter 9).

It may prove helpful to begin with a few words on typefounding, type size, the parts of a piece of type, and spacing material.

First, typefounding in its simplest terms is as follows. The reversed design of each character is cut on the end of a bar of steel to form a *punch* which is then driven into a slab of copper to make a *matrix*. This matrix forms the face of a mould into which molten metal is poured and a type cast. A single piece of type is called a *sort*.

The invention of this process belongs to the fifteenth century and is, in effect, the invention of printing from movable types. Although we do not know exactly how the first typefounders worked, their methods cannot have been substantially different from our present-day hand founding.

Secondly, type size or measurement may be described in a word or two. In Britain and America the *point system* is employed. This is not exactly related to any other scale but 72 points approximately equal 1 inch (actually .9962). Therefore six lines of 12 pt type will occupy a depth of 1 inch. This measurement is the depth of the body on which the typeface is cast. Some faces are large on the body, some small – depending on the length of the *ascending* and *descending* strokes (*extruders*) of the *lower-case* letters. Typographical material is made to the point system so that type, ornaments, spaces, *leads* and *rules* are all exactly related to each other. The following alphabets are set in the 10 pt size:

PLANTIN 110: abcdefghijklmnopqrstuvwxyz

IMPRINT: abcdefghijklmnopqrstuvwxyz

BEMBO: abcdefghijklmnopqrstuvwxyz

This also demonstrates how the size of the face on the *body* affects the alphabet length and consequently the number of words that can be set in a given length of line.

Finally, the names given to the various parts of a printing type are best described visually. Opposite is a drawing of a normal type and beneath this two italic types. For instance, if the face over-reaches its body, the overhanging parts (*kerns*) are designed to rest on the shoulders of adjacent types. This is common in most italic founts.

The position and number of *nicks* on a type vary from fount to fount. In this way the nicks help to distinguish one fount from another of the same size. Also, within the same fount, an extra nick may appear on the *small capitals* in order to distinguish between a small

1. *Face*
2. *Counter*
3. *Bevel*
4. *Shoulder*
5. *Front*
6. *Nick*
7. *Feet*
8. *Groove*
9. *Body, Shank*
10. *Pin-mark*
11. *Back*
12. *Height-to-paper*
13. *Size (depth)*
14. *Set (width)*

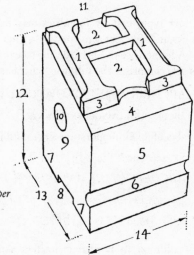

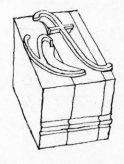

ABOVE: *The nomenclature of a piece of type*
LEFT: *Italic types showing characters with kerns*

capital I and an arabic numeral I; between a small capital O, a roman lower-case o and an arabic numeral zero.

Type cast by the Monotype machine has one rectangular nick and does not have a groove in the *foot*.

33

Other types cast by foundries may have a variety of nicks and two feet separated by a groove.

A fount of 10 pt Ehrhardt, the face in which this book is set, comprises the following characters:

ABCDEFGHIJKLMNOPQRSTUVWXYZ

ABCDEFGHIJKLMNOPQRSTUVWXYZ

abcdefghijklmnopqrstuvwxyz   fifflffflffiffl&æœ

1234567890?'""!:;-.,()[]*†‡&

ABCDEFGHIJKLMNOPQRSTUVWXYZ

abcdefghijklmnopqrstuvwxyz   fifflffflffiffl&æœ

1234567890?'""!;:-.,()[]&

In addition to normal characters some founts have alternative italic letters called *swash characters*. Below are Garamond swash characters and special sorts. They are not included in the normal italic fount.

A B C D E F G H J M P T
V Ex Na Ne Ni No Nu QU
Qu Ra Re Ri Ro Ru e q₂ k m
v ij z as ct et fr gg gy is ll sp st sa ſa
ſc ſe ſi ſo ſs ß ſt ſu ſſa ſſe ſſi ſſo ſſu ta
tt us zy nt

Spacing material is not included in a fount of type. It is bought by weight and is cheaper than type. The height of a *space* is approximately 9 pts less than type-height. This ensures that spaces do not pick up ink and print. Whilst different faces of the same size can use the same spacing material, each size of type must have its own set of spaces. However, it is quite a simple matter to space out a few words set in 24 pt types with 12 pt spaces using two of each space. Taking a 12 pt fount as an example spacing material is made in the following sizes (dimensions in points):

em quadrat or *mutton* $= 12 \times 12$
en quadrat or *nut* $= 12 \times 6$
thick space $= 12 \times 4$
middle space $= 12 \times 3$
thin space $= 12 \times 2.5$ (approx)
hair space $= 12 \times 1$ (approx)

In addition to type-metal hair spaces they may also be made of brass in one point thickness and in copper of half-a-point thickness. Both sizes are required to make an even, visual spacing of capital letters.

In addition to em quadrats (12 pts $\times$ 12 pts) spacing material is made in the following multiples (dimensions in points):

$$12 \times 24 \qquad 12 \times 36 \qquad 12 \times 48$$

which are respectively called two-em, three-em and four-em quadrats. Quadrats of 24 pt and larger sizes are called *quotations* and are cast hollow or with only a framework of metal inside. Their dimensions are based on the 12 pt em, and are made in several sizes up to 6 ems $\times$ 9 ems ($= 72$ pts $\times$ 108 pts).

For each fount of type you will need a separate *case* and these, for small founts, are simple wooden trays divided into 42 equal compartments – the tray itself measuring something like 12 $\times$ 10 inches. The distribution of characters in these cases is best left to the individual printer. It may be found convenient to put capital and lower-case letters of a fount standing face upwards in the same compartment (divided by a short length of *reglet*). In this way you will be able to get all the roman capitals and small letters, figures and punctuation marks and diphthongs and *ligatures* and spaces into one case and still have compartments empty for border units, decorations or small blocks. Then, if you increase the quantity of a particular fount, the pieces of reglet can be removed and the lower-case characters laid out in a separate case.

Larger cases are made with a special layout of compartments varying in size for the lower-case letters. The arrangement is designed for quickness of composition and only becomes your concern if you decide to set up whole pages of type matter. I will assume that the printing of books is not one of your first intentions and therefore recommend the buying of small founts known as *card founts*.

Up to and including the 12 pt size a card fount comprises the following characters:

12 pt *roman* capitals, lower-case and figures:

10 A	16 a	4 J	6 j	8 S	12 s
6 B	8 b	4 K	6 k	8 T	12 t
6 C	8 c	8 L	14 l	6 U	10 u
6 D	8 d	6 M	8 m	4 V	6 v
12 E	20 e	8 N	12 n	6 W	8 w
6 F	10 f	8 O	14 o	4 X	4 x
6 G	8 g	6 P	8 p	6 Y	8 y
6 H	10 h	4 Q	4 q	2 Z	4 z
8 I	16 i	8 R	10 r		

CHARACTER	1	2	3	4	5	6	7	8	9	0
QUANTITY	8	8	6	6	6	6	6	6	8	8

CHARACTER	&	£	?	!	-	,	.	;	:	'
QUANTITY	4	4	6	11	6	18	18	8	8	8

The number of characters differ in large sizes of card founts. For instance in the 18 pt size of roman capitals, lower-case and figures the following characters will be found:

3 A	5 a	2 J	2 j	3 S	4 s
2 B	3 b	2 K	2 k	3 T	4 t
2 C	3 c	3 L	5 l	2 U	3 u
2 D	3 d	2 M	3 m	2 V	2 v
4 E	7 e	3 N	4 n	2 W	2 w
2 F	4 f	3 O	4 o	1 X	2 x
2 G	3 g	3 P	3 p	2 Y	3 y
2 H	3 h	1 Q	1 q	1 Z	1 z
3 I	5 i	3 R	4 r		

CHARACTER	1	2	3	4	5	6	7	8	9	0
QUANTITY	3	2	2	2	2	2	2	2	3	3

CHARACTER	&	£	?	!	-	,	.	;	:	'
QUANTITY	2	1	2	2	4	6	6	2	2	4

From these specifications you can see if one or two card founts will be adequate for your immediate requirements. It would otherwise be more economical to buy larger founts. With each size of type spacing material must be ordered.

If your plans for printing are not yet formed and you wish to begin on an experimental basis I would suggest you purchase two complete card founts each of say 12, 18 and 24 point roman and one complete card fount each of 12, 18 and 24 point italic – all of the one face you have chosen to live with.

The type suppliers' lists and catalogues which are mentioned in Chapter 9 will not be too helpful unless you know what a few lines of Bembo or Plantin or Bodoni may look like on the page. It is the practice of some publishers to state the name of the typeface in which their books are printed and such information is usually to be found on the *verso* of the *title-page*. You may find this helpful in getting to know more about type designs and identifying them. Also, a number of book-printers issue type specimen books and some of these, like Mackays', can be bought (see page 120).

You already have an idea of what Ehrhardt (Mono-type series 453) looks like from reading the text of this book but you may not realize that there is spacing between the lines of type. Line spacing is known as *leading*. The purpose of additional spacing between the lines is to increase the legibility of the typeface – it helps your eye to keep to the line it is reading and to find with ease the beginning of the next line below. Short lines are of course easier to read than long ones, but this can go too far and cause frequent breaks in words. The page with many hyphens at the ends of lines begins to look unsightly. You will find that good design de-pends on a delicate balance of typographical factors.

At the end of this chapter will be found a few speci-

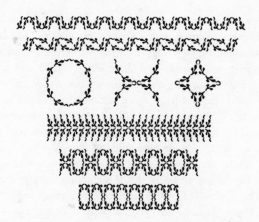

economic and aesthetic considerations. The typographical craftsman should have sufficient experience and skill in his hands to cut with some confidence an alteration on the face of a type. For instance the removal of the 'accent' on this flower ( ) may be desirable in certain instances although it would not justify the cutting of special matrices.

[45]

A page from A Suite of Fleurons *showing Monotype flower 468-9 in use*

mens of settings. Some of these are reproductions from historical sources, some from contemporary sources and some new settings to demonstrate the effects of leading on legibility and the effects of good and bad spacing of words. You will also see that the re-cutting of some fine historical types has not always been successful. I hope that the brief historical notes concerning some of the designs will encourage you to become involved in a more detailed study of typography.

With your own press you have the unique advantage of controlling in every detail the style of the printed page. Unlimited experiments can be carried out with different papers and inks and with different ways of setting and arranging the types; but you will find it very expensive and wasteful to change faces. If at the beginning you choose to buy an odd sort of face you will find its peculiarities, which may have been attractive at first sight, become more and more of an eyesore as you grow familiar with them and compare them with the beauty of traditional letter forms.

In addition to the basic typeface which you choose for your press, one or more of the display types shown on page 56 may be useful and will help you to add a touch of personal distinction to your printing. Whichever display face you choose to supplement and embellish your work it should be most carefully and sparingly used. One line on a title-page is the kind of restraint needed.

You may also want to buy some ornamental border units which can be used singly or in groups, or as complete borders of one sort or of many sorts combined. Before choosing ornaments perhaps I can persuade you to consult a demonstration of printers' flowers or

The Half Iron

DEVISED BY

X'TOPHER BRADSHAW

& JOHN RYDER

A FORM OF PROPOSAL

APRIL 1955

A typical Miniature Press setting. Christopher Bradshaw played an important part in the making of the original edition of Printing for Pleasure *at the Chiswick Press in 1954.*

fleurons which I made in the form of a small book, *A Suite of Fleurons*, first published in 1956 and reissued in 1976 by The Bodley Head under the title *Flowers and Flourishes*. Incidentally all the examples shown in *A Suite of Fleurons* were first set at the Miniature Press, my own press at home, and proofed on an Adana quarto press. The illustration on page 39 is from *A Suite of Fleurons* and it shows the versatility of one very simple flower unit.

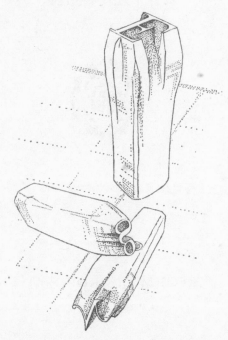

Three of Baskerville's punches now at the University Printing House, Cambridge

SPECIMENS
OF SETTINGS IN A
VARIETY
OF TYPE DESIGNS
AND
SOME DISPLAY
FACES

Sed de his et diximus aliâs satis multa ; et saepe dicemus:nũc autem ;quoniam iam quotidie ferè accidit postea,q̃ e Sicilia ego, et tu reuersi sumus;ut de Aetnae incendiis interrogaremus ab iis, quibus notum est illa nos satis diligenter perspexisse ; ut ea tandem molestia careremus;placuit mi hi eum sermonem conscribere ; quem cum Bernardo parente habui paucis post diebus, q̃ rediissemus; ad quem reiiciendi essent ii, qui nos deinceps quippiam de Aetna postularent. Itaq; confeci librũ; quo uterq; nostrum cõmuniter uteretur: nã cum essemus in Noniano ; et pater se (ut solebat) ante atrium in ripam Pluuici contulisset;accessi ad eũ progresso iam in meridianas horas die:ubi ea, quae locuti sum⁹ inter nos,ferè ista sũt.Tibi uero nũc orationé utriusq; nostrũ,tanq̃ habeatur,

A ii

cit: ex quo fit, ut loca quaeque maritima maxime terraemotibus subiecta sint, parum mediterranea. Quod si etiam in sulfuris venas venti furentes inciderint, tum incendia suscitantur sane non difficulter, quoniam et in sulfure concipiendi permagna ignis vis inest et venti etiam aliena succendunt vi sua. Haec autem tu ut in Aetna accidant omnia, vide, quippe, ut modo tute dixisti, quae mare in radicibus habeat, quae sulfurea sit, quae cavernosa, seu quod natura ita fuerit semper ipsa, seu quod salo aliquando subexesa ventos admiserit aestuantes, per quos idonea flammae materies incenderetur. Habes, unde incendia oriantur Aetnae tuae; habe nunc quomodo etiam orta perdurent. In quo quidem nolo ego te illud admirari, quod vulgus solet: magnum esse scilicet tantas flammas, tam immensos ignes post hominum memoriam semper habuisse, quo alerentur. Quid est enim magnum ipsi magistrae rerum omnium et pa-

Nyctipolon:perche di nocte di lontano riluc
simo e in Actica.In ogni luogho recente & no
benche in Italia ha piu odore & e biancho.La
nūtii la primauera.Et ne luoghi tiepidi piu ā
che e chiamata Porporina.Dipoi laFiameggi
te saluaticha.El Codiamino e due uolte lann
uerno & lastate.Piu serotino de sopradecti e
talia chome habbiamo decto per le Rose.Et i
sto e fiore di Cipolle saluatiche & altro che q
nanthe Melanthio & de saluatichi Helichrys
monia.Dipoi el gladiolo cioe coltelluccio acc
Rosa & prima mancha excepto che laDimest
biancha & lo Enanthe:Ma questa se suelta sp
ghi tiepidi.Ha lodore de fiori delle uiti & inc
ca fiore diuino.Del Hyacintho e doppia fauc
ciullo amato dApolline:o del sangue daIace:
no figura di greche lectere quello significāti.l
tile & el gambo anchora sottile:ma duro.Di
glono lunguéto di uaso doro elquale chiama
niuolentia & alla gloria della uita.Questi sor
el Lichno elsioř digioue & unaltra specie digis
Phrygio:ma molto bello e el Pothos.Questo
del Hyacintho.Laltro ha fiore biancho:elqu
lastate.Nellaučtunno e la terza spetie del Gi
sanza odore & laltro odorifero. Tutti escon fi

❡ I believe in the earth, and in the silver moon: & I believe in day & night, & in the seasons, summer and winter, & spring and autumn; and

❡ I believe and I see that as the earth turns upon itself we pass into the light and wake to life & die downward into darkness and the sleep of rest, and that we are one in life and sleep with the earth's self; and

❡ I believe & see that as the earth, turning upon itself, whirls round the sun, the earth wakes to life in spring, to the full pomp of summer, and dies rhythmically downward

Lo! I must tell a tale of chivalry;
For while I muse, the lance points slantingly
Athwart the morning air: some lady sweet,
Who cannot feel for cold her tender feet,
From the worn top of some old battlement
Hails it with tears, her stout defender sent:

ABOVE: *The Doves Press version of Nicolas Jenson's roman type* (shown opposite) *together with six lines from Morris's* The Poems of John Keats *set in the Golden typeface which was also intended as a version of Jenson's fifteenth-century Venetian model.*

own want of the same. Has he a defect of temper that unfits him to live in society? Thereby he is driven to entertain himself alone and acquire habits of self-help; and thus, like the wounded oyster, he mends his shell with pearl.

Our strength grows out of our weakness. The indignation which arms itself with secret forces does not awaken until we are pricked and stung and sorely assailed. A great man is always willing to be little. Whilst he sits on the cushion of advantages, he goes to sleep. When he is pushed, tormented, defeated, he has a chance to learn something; he has been put on his wits, on

51

ABOVE: *John Bell's original types*
RIGHT: *The Monotype version series 341*

FOURNIER'S FLOWERS

Pierre-Simon Fournier first began to cut punches for his own typefoundry in Paris, *c.* 1736. He died in 1768 having successfully devoted his life to this particular branch of typography, but he died not without some bitterness concerning his constant though fruitless effort to overcome a trade prejudice which denied him the right to print.

For some of the flowers in his first specimen book Fournier drew inspiration from Luce's miniature *Epreuve* of 1740 but the majority of them showed originality and skill. It is interesting to note that he eschewed the splendid vine leaves and arabesques of the sixteenth century.

Fournier's flowers earned him the admiration of the world. His second specimen book, *Modéles des Caractères de l'Imprimerie*, printed by Jean-Joseph Barbou in 1742, contains 118 *vignettes*: his *Les Caractères de l'Imprimerie* of 1764 contains 377 *vignettes* and many of these designs were quickly copied in other European foundries.

[39]

To David Garrick, Esq.

Garrick, I've read your Fools' Petition,
And thank you for the composition;
Tho' few will credit all you say,
Yet 'tis a friendly part you play;
A part which you perform with ease;
Whate'er you act is sure to please!
But give me leave, on this occasion,
To make one little observation:
Tho' no good reason is assigned,
At least not any I can find,
Why I should be *deaf, dumb,* or *blind;*
Yet since it was resolv'd above
By this same Fool-obeying Jove,
I must not speak, or hear, or see,
Surely to soften the decree,
He might have left the *choice* to *me.*
Were that the case, I would dispense
With sight, and wit, and eloquence,
Still to retain my fav'rite sense:
For grant, my friend, we should admit,

ABOVE: *Giambattista Bodoni's original types, printed by Giovanni Mardersteig.* RIGHT: *Monotype version series 135*

These lines are set in Bodoni 135, the Monotype version cut in 1925. It is not like a Bodoni design and compares unfavourably with the typeface shown opposite. These opening lines come from *The Poetical Works of Philip Dormer Stanhope*, published by Elkin Mathews & Marrot in 1927 and printed in January of that year by Mardersteig at his Officina Bodoni in Montagnola.

It may be interesting to note that in 1925 a type design was cut and proofed by Monotype and labelled: designation 135. This trial cutting was closer to original Bodoni types than the version shown here but unfortunately was never produced. It may also be noted that Bodoni was not included in Stanley Morison's *A Tally of Types* (1953) to which account Brooke Crutchley added a note to say that the Monotype version was based on the American Type Founders' own revival – which may sound strange when we consider that the original punches and matrices were (and are) extant at Parma and that Giovanni Mardersteig was currently printing with types from this original material at Montagnola.

throughout *The Savoy's* run of eight issues. The first number was intended for Christmas publication in 1896 but actually appeared in January 1896, and the seven issues which followed were all published that year. It began as a quarterly but ended as a monthly from July onwards. Ernest Dowson, as a regular contributor, wrote to Smithers, 'I hope it will succeed as well in its monthly aspect as I presume it has as a quarterly. May the hair of John Lane grow green with envy!' (*The Letters of Ernest Dowson*, Cassell, 1967). Smithers was declared bankrupt in 1900 and Lane took over the remaining stock of *The Savoy* (300 of the original edition of 2,000 copies) together with the copyright of Beardsley's work – Aubrey Beardsley had died in 1898.

In 1903 The Bodley Head issued a 32-page booklet *Aubrey Beardsley & The Yellow Book*. In this were listed all thirteen issues of *The Yellow Book* and all eight issues of *The Savoy*, together with the Beardsley novel, *Under the Hill*, which Smithers had published as *Venus and Tannhäuser*, a variant text, bearing neither publisher's nor printer's names and supposedly but doubtfully limited to 300 copies.

The *Westminster Gazette* said of the Beardsley drawings in the first issue of *The Yellow Book*: '. . . we do not know that anything would meet the case except a

ABOVE: *A setting in Ehrhardt, Monotype series 453, 11 point without leading and with poor word-spacing.*
OPPOSITE: *Setting in the same size and typeface but with leading and with some attention paid to word-spacing. Taken from a booklet printed at the Stellar Press.*

throughout *The Savoy's* run of eight issues. The first number was intended for Christmas publication in 1895 but actually appeared in January 1896, and the seven issues which followed were all published that year. It began as a quarterly but ended as a monthly from July onwards. Ernest Dowson, as a regular contributor, wrote to Smithers, 'I hope it will succeed as well in its monthly aspect as I presume it has as a quarterly. May the hair of John Lane grow green with envy!' (*The Letters of Ernest Dowson*, Cassell, 1967). Smithers was declared bankrupt in 1900 and Lane took over the remaining stock of *The Savoy* (300 of the original edition of 2,000 copies) together with the copyright of Beardsley's work – Aubrey Beardsley had died in 1898.

In 1903 The Bodley Head issued a 32-page booklet *Aubrey Beardsley & The Yellow Book*. In this were listed all thirteen issues of *The Yellow Book* and all eight issues of *The Savoy*, together with the Beardsley novel, *Under the Hill*, which Smithers had published as *Venus and Tannhäuser*, a variant text, bearing neither publisher's nor printer's names and supposedly but doubtfully limited to 300 copies.

The *Westminster Gazette* said of the Beardsley drawings in the first issue of *The Yellow Book*: '. . . we do not know that anything would meet the case except a short Act of Parliament to make this kind of thing illegal.' A portrait of Mrs Patrick Campbell was particularly referred to. This indictment sounds more like a reference to the *Lysistrata* illustrations, which, until the

The several articles by James Wardrop published by Oliver Simon in *Signature* are quite indispensable – as is A. F. Johnson's 'Catalogue of Italian Writing-Books of the Sixteenth Century' also published in *Signature*. The wealth of articles and introductions written by Stanley Morison require particular mention; his researches and interest in the subject of writing-books form the basis of the present work. Giovanni Mardersteig, for his researches and his impeccable work on facsimile-making, earns my greatest admiration.

'The whole question of bibliographical descriptions of the Italian writing-books and the interrelationship of the various writers, their borrowings from each other and use of each other's blocks, is so tortuous as to require a prolonged and detailed study.' Thus wrote James Wells in his introduction to a reprint of Tagliente's *Opera* of 1525 published in 1952 by the Newberry Library, Chicago. James Wells makes it sound as though it could be a friendly borrowing but in fact there were some bitter rivalries. James Mosley describes conflict between Cresci and Palatino in his article 'Trajan Revived' published in *Alphabet* in 1964. 'In mid-sixteenth century,' James Mosley writes, 'calligraphers were as touchy and jealous as opera singers.' A little earlier in the century

ABOVE: *Setting in 11 point Bembo, Monotype series 270, with leading.* OPPOSITE: *The same text set in 10 point Plantin, Monotype series 110, with three times as much leading as in the Bembo setting. Bembo is the Monotype version of Griffo's De Aetna typeface. The text quoted here is from the author's* Lines of the Alphabet, *1960.*

The several articles by James Wardrop published by Oliver Simon in *Signature* are quite indispensable – as is A. F. Johnson's 'Catalogue of Italian Writing-Books of the Sixteenth Century' also published in *Signature*. The wealth of articles and introductions written by Stanley Morison require particular mention; his researches and interest in the subject of writing-books form the basis of the present work. Giovanni Mardersteig, for his researches and his impeccable work on facsimile-making, earns my greatest admiration.

'The whole question of bibliographical descriptions of the Italian writing-books and the inter-relationship of the various writers, their borrowings from each other and use of each other's blocks, is so tortuous as to require a prolonged and detailed study.' Thus wrote James Wells in his introduction to a reprint of Tagliente's *Opera* of 1525 published in 1952 by the Newberry Library, Chicago. James Wells makes it sound as though it could be a friendly borrowing but in fact there were some bitter rivalries. James Mosley describes conflict between Cresci and Palatino in his article 'Trajan Revived' published in *Alphabet* in 1964. 'In mid-sixteenth century,' James Mosley writes, 'calligraphers were as touchy and jealous as opera singers.' A little earlier in the century Arrighi and da Carpi seem to have had problems which are now difficult to unravel. Licence granted to Arrighi was withdrawn and given to da Carpi. Apparently identical blocks appear in one book and then reappear in a

DISPLAY TYPES

ABCDEFGH

Bell Roman, 36 pt, Monotype 341

IJKLM

Bembo Roman, 48 pt, Monotype 270

NOPQ

Castellar, 48 pt, Monotype 600

rstuv&wxyz

Scotch Roman, 36 pt, Monotype 46

ABCDEFG

Walbaum, 36 pt, Monotype 374

[4]

How to Handle and
Arrange Movable Types

The setting or composing of type to be printed on a power-driven press is a complicated and highly skilled procedure. Before a man becomes efficient in this, years of apprenticeship and practical experience are necessary.

However the knowledge required to print on a flatbed hand-press is easily acquired. The simplest form of machine and the simplest method of setting will, in practice, explain the whole technique and lead you to set up more complicated jobs and use any of the presses mentioned in Chapter 2.

The notes here and in the following chapter are based on the use of an Adana quarto horizontal platen press but the instructions are nevertheless applicable to other machines. Therefore I will assume that you have a press and type already laid out in cases. With the press will be supplied a chase and with the type should be bought spacing material. The following accessories must also be acquired from a printers' supplier (see page 115) before work can commence:

1. Wooden *furniture* (still sold in 36 inch lengths), 24, 36, 48 and 96 point sizes to position the type in the chase.

2. Reglet (thin wood furniture as above), $1\frac{1}{2}$ to 18 point sizes for spacing the lines of type. Reglet is also available in coloured plastic.

3. Leads (still sold in 24 inch lengths), 1, $1\frac{1}{2}$, 2 and 3 point sizes also for spacing the lines of type. Leads of 4 points thickness or more are called *clumps*.

4. *Quoins* (expanding metal or wood blocks) and key to lock up type in the chase.

5. Tweezers for picking small metal types and spaces out of the cases or out of matter set up in the chase. Take care never to touch the face of type with tweezers.

6. *Composing stick* for setting up the type into words or lines before placing them in the chase.

7. Hand-guillotine for cutting leads, brass rule, etc.

8. *Tenon saw* and *mitre block* for cutting wood furniture and reglet.

9. *Lye* for cleaning type and blocks.

Here is a simple method of setting up the types needed to print the example opposite – a cover for a catalogue of prints and drawings.

The types used in this example are Bembo, 24 and 12 point. Types of the 24 pt size are large enough to be set up by hand, word by word, and placed on the table for checking and spacing before being set in the chase. The letters required to set 'First Folio of Houses' may therefore be taken out of the case letter by letter with the right hand and placed in the left hand reading from left to right but upside down (see page 60).

When the first lines are placed in the chase the right way round but reading from right to left, the correct

First
Folio of Houses

RICHMOND, PETERSHAM, HAM
AND TWICKENHAM

THE MINIATURE PRESS

RICHMOND

Specimen setting for catalogue cover

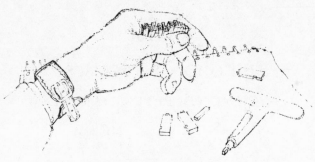

Setting types in the hand

position for printing will be achieved. Set each line in the middle of the chase. Fill up the remainder of these lines with spaces and quads of the same point size so that an even pressure will be obtained when locking up the chase (see drawing on page 64). The centring is easily checked with a pair of dividers and the spacing on each side of the type should not completely fill the line. Leave about 12 pts clearance to allow optical centring of the lines after the first proof is taken.

The next two lines are of 12 pt roman capitals. These smaller types will more conveniently be set first in the composing stick (see page 62). The line of type, supported by a length of 6 pt reglet, should be taken out of the stick – using the forefinger and thumb of each hand (see page 63) – and then transferred to the chase. Practice will make the use of a supporting reglet unnecessary for short lines and the feeling for handling type will soon be acquired.

In this way the two final lines of type (in 12 pt roman capitals and 12 pt small capitals) should be set up and transferred to the chase. The *device* of the Miniature Press (in this instance a *line block* made from a drawing)

OAK HOUSE

King Street and The Green, Richmond

ARCHITECT : SIR ROBERT TAYLOR

c. 1760

Specimen setting for catalogue page

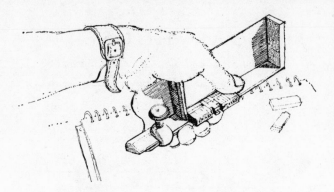

Holding types in the composing stick

can either be put in the bed of the press with the type and inked with colour at the same time as the type is inked with black or omitted from the first setting and printed separately. Careful hand-inking is required if two inks are printed at once. This, and how to obtain the correct position of the block and paper for a second printing in colour, is explained in Chapter 5.

Next the type and block must be placed in the chase. The chase itself fits into the bed of the press where it is secured by screws. The type should be locked with quoins in both directions but the Miniature Press examples reproduced in this book have been set and printed in a simplified way shown in the drawing on page 64. This method would not be adequate for setting a complete page of small type but by starting the first job like this a useful basic set of furniture will be made for all similar jobs including printing from blocks.

The wood furniture and reglet, purchased in 36-inch lengths, must be cut. This is best done on a mitre block with a tenon saw (plastic reglet up to one point is easily cut with strong scissors). Cut the wood in lengths one sixteenth of an inch less than the inside width of the chase so that each piece can be removed easily when putting in or taking out lines of type.

If the block is to be printed with the type some shorter pieces of wood will be needed. The spaces on each side of the block must be filled to exactly the same depth as the block. It will otherwise be impossible to

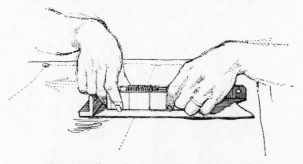

Removing lines of type from the composing stick

secure all the material firmly. Possibly the wood furniture, reglet and leads will not give you the exact depth. The final adjustment should then be made with a piece of card or paper.

The drawing on page 64 shows the setting ready to print. You will notice that quoins are used for making the correct depth of spacing on each side of the block. With quoins a slight turn of the key makes the correct adjustment and saves cutting paper and card of various thicknesses.

When all is ready to be locked up by expanding the quoins with a key see that the types and spaces in each line sit closely together. When locking the chase in one direction only first lock with a very light pressure

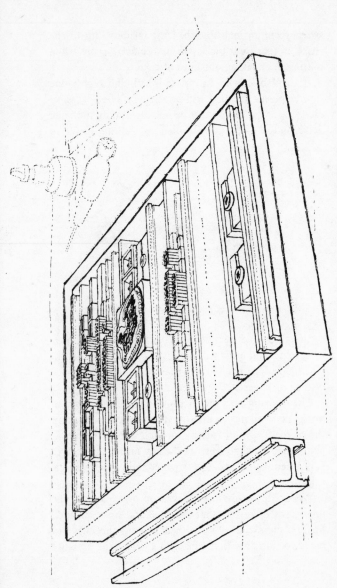

A forme with type and block locked in one direction, using light-weight metal furniture and reglet and then push with forefingers and thumbs each line from its ends towards the middle. At this stage be sure the types are standing exactly upright or they will not print correctly. Next increase the pressure with a slight turn of the key before taking the first proof. Any types standing a fraction higher than the rest will be pressed into their correct seating. This process may be assisted by *planing* the type. To do this place a piece of 72 point wood furniture on the type and tap it gently with a small mallet. Move the piece of furniture over all the type and continue to strike lightly with the mallet. Finally the chase with the type, furniture and blocks (now called a forme) may be locked more tightly.

In the foregoing notes I have not mentioned metal furniture but there are two kinds – ordinary metal and light-weight metal – in addition to quotations which can be used as furniture. After some experience with all these kinds I would say that the most satisfactory set should comprise light-weight metal furniture and reglet. Thin ($1\frac{1}{2}$ pt) reglet placed between light-weight furniture and lines of type will avoid any possibility of the furniture 'bruising' the softer type-metal and all fear of warping will be abolished. A forme largely made up of ordinary metal furniture is very heavy; a forme consisting mainly of wood furniture is light but may suffer from warping and/or bulging. With light-weight metal furniture the advantages of strength and constant shape are combined with that of lightness. Ordinary metal furniture is softer than type-metal and may therefore easily become damaged.

This is the simplified form of type-setting except for one important refinement. The roman capitals here, and indeed in all settings, will need to be spaced. In order to have the same visual space between printed letters, spaces of varying thickness must be inserted between the types. Hence the space to be inserted between H and I or J and L will necessarily be more than between B and O or between P and S and still more than between A and D or P and A. No space at all will be needed between A and V or R and Y. In fact, if the R has a long tail like the Bembo R considerable space will have to go between H and I to make the even, visual space in a word like HISTORY.

HISTORY   without *letter-spacing*

HISTORY   a thin space between each letter

HISTORY   even, visual spacing

The hair spaces inserted between the letters in the third version are: 2, 1½, 1, 1, 1½ and 1 respectively.

The same, of course, applies to italic capitals, but you will probably be satisfied with an even spacing of small capitals:

HISTORY OF QUADRUPEDS   without letter-spacing

HISTORY OF QUADRUPEDS   hair spaces inserted

HISTORY OF QUADRUPEDS   with thin spaces

All is now ready to take a proof. (Directions for inking are given in Chapter 5.) Take the first proof on tissue paper and place this proof on a sheet of white paper so that the printing may be clearly seen. Mark on the proof any adjustments you think should be done. Then take a broad view of the proof to see if the disposition of the lines and block gives a pleasing appearance. Look at the black lines of print and at the white lines of space. Look also at the relationship of the line lengths. Does the message to be conveyed by this print come over clearly? By using different sizes of types a varying emphasis is laid on the different parts of the message. Is this emphasis correct? Again, mark anything to be changed. Then hold the tissue paper proof up to the light and fold it so that the longest line of letters is exactly halved. This will then show you whether or not all the lines and the block are centred. Again, mark anything which requires to be moved. Now unlock the forme and correct according to your remarks on the proof.

When all adjustments have been made take another proof on tissue paper to check the centring of lines and then take a third proof on opaque paper on which you can draw in the proposed margins and examine the final appearance. You are then ready to prepare for printing as described in the following chapter.

Let us examine very briefly the reverse procedure known as *distribution*. This means returning the types and spaces to their respective compartments in the cases, which must be done with the same care as composition or chaos will soon overtake any further attempts at composing.

First the type must be cleaned. To do this take two or three 'dry' impressions until the print is grey. Then wipe over the type and block (and, incidentally, any spaces or furniture which may have picked up ink) with a nylon rag moistened – just the part you are using – with lye. This will clean only the printing surface of the types and block and the operation may be completed with a brush. Pour a little lye on to the brush (an old toothbrush will do) and scrub over the types gently. Do not use any kind of rag which will easily shed fibres – wool and cotton are useless.

Now unlock the forme and remove some of the furniture so that the lines of type can be easily taken from the bed of the press and placed on the table. As in the reverse procedure of composing a strip of reglet will make it easy to handle lines of type. Take up one word at a time and distribute the letters into the correct compartments of the cases. Do the same with the spaces and quads. When all types and blocks have been removed from the press take out the remaining furniture and clean the bed of the press.

Woodcut by Jost Amman for a sixteenth-century playing card suite depicting dabbers or inkballs.

[5]
How to Ink
and Take Impressions

An early method of inking *woodcuts* and type was by means of a *dabber* or *inkball* shaped like a flattened hemisphere on a handle. The inkball is padded and covered with leather and is held in the hand. By dabbing and rocking this simple instrument first on an ink-plate and then on the type a more or less even film of ink is spread ready for the pressman to lay-on paper and take an impression. The trade-mark of several early printers showed a pair of inkballs held by a man, a rampant lion or a dragon and the device is occasionally redrawn for use today.

This method of dabbing did not give a perfectly even distribution of ink and therefore the *roller* needed to be invented. Most hand-presses have more than one roller to ensure even inking and commercial machines have systems of rollers and *riders* (a name given to rollers which ride on the backs of other rollers to aid the distribution of ink). The Adana quarto horizontal platen press's inking system is very simple and consists of two rollers, joined to the platen by curved arms which move them from ink-plate to type and from type to ink-plate as the press is opened and shut. Therefore the inking becomes automatic and the operator has only to lay-on and take-off paper with one hand and operate the press with a lever held in the other hand.

Before examining the automatic inking system let us look at hand-inking. This method is more likely to be of use to those who print purely for pleasure. The two rollers are easily detached from the press by unscrewing the bolts, one on each side of the platen. Once the rollers are off, the bed of the press is easy to get at both for setting the type and for inking with a hand-roller. The following items of equipment will be needed:

1. Composition or plastic hand-roller, about 100 mm wide.
2. Tin or tube of black jobbing ink.
3. A square of thick glass measuring a little more than the width of your roller for rolling out the ink.
4. Palette knife for mixing and spreading ink.
5. Tissue paper.
6. Proofing paper (any cheap paper).
7. Tinting medium (for mixing transparent inks).
8. Tins or tubes of coloured inks.

Squeeze out a very small blob of ink onto the glass plate. Work it thinly over an area about equal to the square of the roller's width with the palette knife. Then roll out the ink with the roller. Roll from top to bottom and bottom to top and from left to right and right to left making a very thin, even area of ink. Then take the roller gently but firmly over the type. Roll in the direction of the lines of type and diagonally, taking care not to bump the roller across the type from one line to the next. Here a little practical experience is worth many pages of instructions. You will soon get the feeling for handling the roller. It does not in the least matter how much mess you make the first time so long as you understand the source of error and correct your mistakes.

Now take an impression on a sheet of paper. This should be a sheet of the paper on which the job is to be printed. Use only a slight pressure on the arm of the press and adjust the pressure screw and locking nut to this slight pressure. Take out your first sheet and examine the back for depth of impression. Only a slight embossing should appear on this side of the paper and it should be even over the whole print. Adjust the pressure screw until correct depth of impression is obtained.

After taking the first print, and without re-inking, print onto the top sheet of the *platen packing*. This will give you a grey impression which will not smear too easily (powdered chalk will dry it immediately) and will allow you to draw the required margins around this printed area. Use two adjacent margins as guides for inserting the paper which can quite easily be held in position with the left hand until the grippers of the press automatically take over. They come into operation when the platen reaches the vertical position.

Certain adjustments may need to be made in order to get a good print. First there is the depth of impression which I have already mentioned. The screw on the back of the platen controls this. Then it may be found that the depth of impression varies. If the impression near the hinge of the platen is deep, then there is too much packing on the platen; if shallow, then there is too little packing. This must be adjusted before the grey print is put onto the top sheet. The quantity of ink must also be controlled and should be right by the time you have made three or four prints. Any tendency to greyness will show that there is too little ink. On the other hand over-inked types will not print with clean, sharp edges. To reduce the quantity of ink that the roller will pick up run the fully inked roller once or twice over a sheet of clean paper. This will reduce the thickness of the film of ink very slightly and the process may be repeated (using a clean sheet of paper each time if necessary) until exactly the right thickness of ink film is obtained.

The two-colour example shown on page 59 can be printed in one operation or two, according to the skill exercised in inking. If you print both colours in one operation a second ink-plate and roller will be required. It is not particularly difficult to print the two colours together but care must be taken not to let the roller with red ink touch the type. I would suggest using the black roller first. You can then carefully wipe the block with a rag if it has picked up ink from the black roller. Then put the red roller onto the middle of the block and roll very carefully towards one edge and back again to the opposite edge. Now the finished print can be taken with one impression.

If the job is to be done in two separate printings, (and this is essential where a block is close to the type), set up and print the typematter in black as already described. Then set the block in the chase as near as you can measure to the correct position. Ink the block and take a proof on a sheet of tissue paper laid on the platen in exactly the same position as the sheets you have printed in black only. Place this tissue proof over one of the black prints and you will see whether the block is in the required position or not. Make any adjustment required either by moving the block in the chase or by altering the guide marks on the platen packing. The same adjustments for depth and evenness of impression and quantity of ink for printing blocks apply as for printing type. Where blocks and type are printed together it will be found that the *process-engraver* has made the block a fraction less than type height. It is a simple matter to increase the height of the block by pasting a thin piece of card on the bottom of the mount and perfecting the adjustment with pieces of paper cut from, say, a thin sticky label.

The small block from the example on page 59 will present no difficulties in preparation (*make-ready*) and printing. When it comes to blocks of larger sizes – especially if there are areas of solid black to be printed – a more complicated make-ready may be needed. In addition to adjusting the height of a block by sticking card and paper on the bottom of the mount (this is called *underlay*), it is possible to make a part of the block print more definitely than another part by sticking paper onto the platen packing itself (this is called *overlay*). When you have printed a grey impression on the platen packing you will know exactly where the thin paper overlay is needed. The thicker the paper you use the more heavy will be the impression of those parts. To avoid a hard edge, tear rather than cut the paper, or the parts of the block extending just beyond the area (of the print on the platen) covered by the overlay paper will not print at all – or very faintly. Practice in very careful tearing and sticking on of this overlay will be needed before you can make blocks print exactly as you want them to print. Yet you will be astonished to see how easy it is to get perfect results from small delicately engraved blocks.

Hand-inking is particularly satisfying when printing blocks and type together and in the same colour. It is quite impossible for a commercial machine, such as the one employed in printing this book, to vary the quantity of ink on a page. When it comes to hand-inking the roller can be taken three or four times over the block and but once over the type – or the other way about if the block is lighter in colour than the type.

A few words on colour may be useful. My ink store until recently consisted of $\frac{1}{4}$lb tins of black, white, red, yellow and blue. If you use white ink, as I did, to reduce the strength of a colour, the resultant mixture is opaque. Also the exact shade visualized for a particular job could not always be made up from these primaries. It is particularly useful to know that you can mix artists' oil colours (which you can buy in very small tubes) with your printing ink. Use only a minute quantity of oil-paint – just enough to turn the colour of your printing ink to the required shade – and if you want to print a transparent tint background, do not mix with white ink – use a tinting medium. This is the 'body' of normal printing ink without the pigment added. Take a little tinting medium, just as you would any ordinary ink, and mix the desired colour into it thoroughly with a palette knife. This will give you a thin, transparent tint over which may be printed type or a block in a full-bodied colour or in black.

If you should ever want to print a hundred invitations, labels or bookplates it would almost certainly be worth your while to employ the automatic inking system. All the preliminaries of setting, proofing, correcting and make-ready will apply as for hand-inking. Then thoroughly clean the rollers with a nylon rag partly soaked with lye and connect the arms to the platen by screwing in the bolts. While the press is open and the

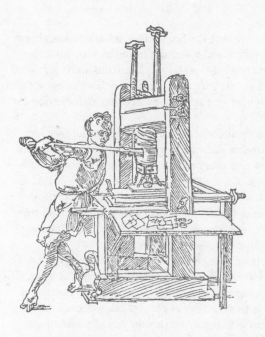

May we have the pleasure of inviting
Mr & Mrs Max Reinhardt
to visit?

THE MINIATURE PRESS
Richmond, Surrey

Simple setting for an invitation card with a drawing
after Albrecht Dürer

rollers are over the bed transfer ink which has already been mixed and rolled out from the glass plate to the ink-plate of the press. Work out the ink evenly over the ink-plate first with the hand-roller and then with the rollers of the press by opening and shutting the press.

The quantity of ink on the plate is controlled by the hand-roller and, once correct, it only needs to be maintained after every ten or more impressions – depending on how much ink is being used for each print. A very quick working can be achieved if you get someone to maintain the ink supply for you with the hand-roller whilst your attention is given to laying-on and taking-off the paper and working the press.

It is very important, whatever you are printing, to *interleave* each newly printed sheet with a piece of scrap paper or tissue. You will otherwise risk *set-off* – that is to say, some of the wet ink will come off onto the backs of the sheets in your pile of printed paper.

Although the inking systems of the various presses described in Chapter 2 are all different the principles of inking type and blocks remain the same. The Albion, Columbian and Washington presses employ hand-inking as described above. The Adana quarto press is also suitably designed for hand-inking though it has attachments for automatic inking. The vertical platen presses (Peerless, Model, Adana) are not designed for hand-inking. They have the bed in the vertical position and a circular ink-plate arranged above the bed. Ink is transferred from a mixing plate to the circular ink-plate which revolves as the press is operated thus aiding an even distribution of the ink. The advantage of these vertical platens is the speed at which they can be made to print. The quality of printing is not necessarily impaired but it may be. It is certainly not possible with a vertical platen press to do any of the special inking performances described in this chapter.

Hand-rollers and those of the presses need careful treatment. Their composition is a sensitive impressionable substance and the only way to make them do good service is to keep them clean and always to hang them up when not in use. They must not be left inked and standing on the ink-plate or in contact with type or blocks.

Ordinary black jobbing ink is slow-drying and may be left on the roller for a day or two providing the roller is hung up and not in contact with anything. But rollers which have been used for colours or for a quick-drying black ink must be cleaned immediately after use.

Rollers are easily mis-shapen by heat and damaged by water. Nevertheless the life of a composition roller will probably be anything from one to three years and after that period it can be melted and recast. A plastic roller will last longer and will not be damaged by water.

If you use ink in tins, the lids must be replaced immediately after use – not at the end of the printing session. If you use tubes the caps must be screwed on again as soon as the blob of ink is squeezed out. Ink, especially coloured ink, dries quickly forming a thick skin. Once a skin has formed in the tin, keep this skin and obtain ink by digging beneath it with a palette knife.

Your black and colours should be *letterpress* inks. But if you are ambitious and want to print *half-tone blocks* on a hand-press then you will require special

A divergence of press marks or devices: Ark Press (top),
Shoestring Press (left), *Hammer Creek Press*
(right) *and Rampant Lions Press*

ink. Your ink supplier will recommend the correct inks if you tell him your needs.

Lastly we come to paper. The thickness, colour and surface texture of the paper you choose will be governed by personal taste. It is worth your while to buy a really good paper – one on which you can print type and line or wood blocks perfectly. Many papers of good colour and with smooth though not shiny surfaces are available today. If you buy 500 sheets of Imperial Royal paper (635×508 mm) and have this cut to Royal folio (508×318 mm), the resultant 1,000 sheets may supply your needs for quite a while.

After you have been printing for some time, with perhaps already a project for a small book in mind, you may wish to experiment with printing on hand-made papers. This is a special process because the hard, usually sized, surface of such papers will not take ink properly unless the paper is damp. A good description of printing on hand-made paper will be found in Louis Allen's *Printing with the Handpress*, originally privately issued in 1969 and now available through Nostrand Reinhold of New York.

For taking rough proofs use any odd scraps of paper or buy some thin typewriting or duplicating paper. For interleaves tissue paper is very satisfactory; but if this is not available tear up some sheets of old newspaper.

Attractive coloured papers and cards which can be obtained from a number of mills will assist you to make covers and labels, greetings- and invitation-cards and so on. It is perhaps worthwhile noting here that Basingwerk Parchment is obtainable in a toned (ivory) shade and in several colours – deep buff, grey, lichen, suede and blue. If you want to make miniature portfolios, boxes or slip-cases in which to keep *progression proofs* or specimen sheets or printed ephemera from your own or other private presses, I can recommend the fine marbled papers from Sydney Cockerell, Riversdale, Grantchester, Cambridge, England.

ABC
DEFGH
IJK✠MN
OPQRS
TUVW
XYZ

Christmas card by Kenneth Hardacre at his Kit-Cat Press using Michelangelo types by Hermann Zapf.

[6]
Developing a
Taste for Experiment

The simplest machine is sometimes capable of being used in a complex way. This is true of the Adana quarto horizontal platen press. Although the machine itself is quite uncomplicated it may be used in a variety of ways. Many of the experiments which follow are not given as accomplishments in themselves but rather as examples to whet your appetite for this kind of investigation.

One of the simplest and yet extremely useful adaptations of this Adana press is effected by unscrewing and removing the pressure arch. This done it is possible to print a few words (for instance a *caption* to a map or an architectural drawing) on the margins of a sheet of paper of considerable size – a sheet 762 × 508 mm could be easily handled and perfectly printed. Set the type at the hinge-end of the bed so that the grippers make good contact with the paper, and use a hand-roller to ink the type.

Where normal printing is concerned I am in favour of removing the rollers from this flatbed press and employing hand-inking rollers – but the press's own rollers may come in useful for experiment. For instance on my first Adana quarto press (made in 1935) there was only one roller with a circumference of about 203mm (the new model's twin rollers are only 102mm in circumference). This meant that, with a little ingenuity, a block whose design was reversible from left to right (type must be excluded) could be printed by the offset technique. To do this the press is opened so that the roller is close to the hinge of the platen. Thus the block, which is placed as near as possible to the ink-plate, may be carefully hand-inked. On the ink-plate a sheet of paper is placed and stuck down. The press is then carefully and slowly closed to drive the clean roller steadily over the inked block and onto the paper-covered ink-plate where it will leave an 'offset' print of the block. This print will be like the block itself since the impression was first taken on the roller and then transferred from the roller to the paper. From this first impression you can calculate exactly where to lay the papers for further printing so that the offset impression is placed where you want it on the page. Thus the reliefs of coins and tokens can be carefully inked and transferred to paper from the roller. The roller must be wiped clean after each impression because it will never roll over the coin or block in the bed of the press in exactly the same place again and the second printing would be blurred. Whatever object you use must be secured in the press type-high. This can easily be achieved by securing the object with rubber gum onto a piece of wood furniture or block mount. Both inking and offsetting must be done in the lightest possible manner. In this way the most subtle black and grey prints can be made with the high reliefs in solid black and the lower reliefs paler, and with the background reduced to a very soft grey.

I have frequently employed my Adana quarto press to print *spine labels* for books. For some time I experimented in order to find a quick way to set up a number of short lines which must be exactly centred without going to the trouble of setting in the composing stick and *justifying* each line. Eventually the idea of setting type straight out of the case onto a graph-paper bed occurred to me. To do this and to be certain of exact line centring place a sheet of graph-paper in the bed of the press before putting in the furniture. Then place in your short lines of type with three- or four-em quadrats at each end of every line to hold the types steady whilst the complete set of lines is being placed in position. Working with a marked centre line on the graph-paper, every line of type is moved until it occupies as many squares on the left as on the right of this line. A visual allowance can be made for lines ending with a hyphen or a Y or some other letter which does not visually occupy the area of the type body. Leads or reglet for line spacing need not be specially cut – odd lengths will do. Lock up gently (in one direction) with a quoin and take a proof on tissue paper which can be folded across the lines of print so that the first and last letters of the longest line are exactly super-imposed. When all the lines are precisely halved by the same fold (at right angles to the lines of print) then each line is centred and the setting is ready to be printed.

Once you have established your press and become familiar with the equipment and with its normal use, experimental methods may become part of the normal procedure. The hand-roller by itself is quite an important and adaptable tool. With a little experience it is possible to print background tints directly from the roller. Using the tinting medium listed on page 70 delicate transparent colours can be rolled onto part or

A POCKET FOLIO OF

Georgian Houses

IN ENGLAND, WITH DRAWINGS BY

Christopher Chamberlain

The Miniature Press

RICHMOND

Simple setting for a title-page

all of the sheet as required. Different sizes of roller can be used. Or a large roller can be partially inked to suit your particular purpose. A really transparent tint can be rolled onto a printed sheet without fear of obliterating black type or block impressions.

Elsewhere in this book some insistence on careful treatment of rollers is made. In this experimental chapter a little more licence can be allowed. The point is, unless the gelatine composition rollers are kept clean, they become permanently damaged and will very soon need to be recast. The ink hardens and becomes difficult to remove and the usual result is that the surface of the roller becomes pitted. Dampness may cause blistering and subsequent pitting and heat will put the roller out of shape. Should any or all of these 'accidents' befall one of your rollers may I suggest that you turn your misfortune into profit? The 'accidental' surface of the roller may very likely make an interesting print as a background to type or blocks. I have made roller prints which have been successfully *photo-engraved* as line blocks and used as colour backgrounds to drawings where solid or *mechanical tint* backgrounds might have looked dull or out-of-keeping with the drawings themselves.

The natural pattern of pits and blemishes may be augmented and embellished in many ways. For instance a very interesting extra pattern of white lines can be added by scraping the inked roller with a comb. Rotate the roller with one hand and move the teeth of the comb across the surface of the roller with the other hand to create a pattern of waves or zig-zag lines as desired. Another method is to throw or arrange fine grains of ground rice, salt, or sugar on the paper and then run the inked roller over them. A rash of white dots is thus obtained and this may be a useful way of lightening the background block in order to focus attention on some particular part of the illustration to be overprinted. Some experience with these unusual techniques is necessary in order to see just exactly what can be done with them and what value they have.

You may also discover that a lightly inked and lightly impressed block on a rough or a *laid surface* of paper will sometimes give an interesting pattern to the solids. This pattern is caused by the wire-marks of the paper and sometimes also by the *watermark*.

What is so important about these experimental techniques – which may at first seem of interest only to the amateur working at home – is their application to commercial printing. As an example let us just take this last experiment of reduced ink and pressure. I have several times had book covers printed on *cartridge paper* with an open wove linen backing. At first I thought that the linen backing would merely add strength to the book covers and that, by using plenty of ink and sufficient pressure, solid colour could be obtained where required. Of course this is quite true, but by using less ink and pressure a most interesting background pattern is obtained. Knowledge gained through the most simple experiments and applied with some technical skill and sense of design will sometimes produce worthy results.

A vast field of experiment with wide application is open to the printer with a flatbed machine. Careful inking by hand and careful pressure will enable him to print almost anything. For instance, some years ago, just to demonstrate my belief in this claim, I collected some small feathers, dry leaves, green leaves, pieces of bracken and various grasses in their autumn state of ripeness. Though most of them tended to curl at the edges and the dry seed-bearing grass inclined to stand out in all directions, these objects were all successfully inked and printed on paper. In such experiments the inking must be done outside the press (because the very low relief of these 'blocks' would allow the mount to become inked too) and then placed in the bed of the press on a clean mount approximately type-high. Light pressure (which will involve slight crushing) will produce a print with remarkable qualities of solid black and varying grey tones. Different pressures give different results and a second impression is generally somewhat changed from the first impression owing to the crushing involved in each printing. Feathers and grasses will never print twice in exactly the same way but it is quite astonishing how they print to paper their own essential visual qualities.

An alternative method of printing a natural 'block' is to place the leaf (or whatever you please) on a sheet of paper, ink it lightly, place it on another sheet of paper (because the first sheet will have become inked) and take the ink off the leaf with a clean roller. Thus the impression of the leaf can be transferred to wherever you wish. There is a certain amount of skill involved in these techniques but not so much that you cannot acquire it whilst experimenting.

Experimental inking is also possible with vertical platen machines fitted with ink-ducts. The ink-duct can be divided and two or more different inks supplied to the ink-plate and to the rollers at the same time. With care these colours may either be kept separate or blended, and many interesting effects obtained.

It is a pity that few private presses have concerned themselves with experimental techniques since it is here on the amateur's workbench (a place from which the time-sheet and the wage-bill are absent), that experiments can be made and repeated without end and without fear of bankruptcy.

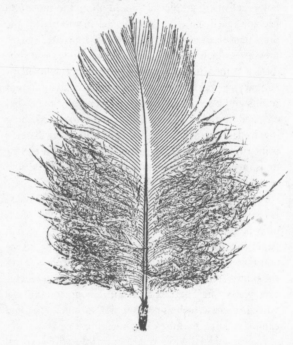

A line block reproduction made from a
'nature print' of a feather
(see page 86)

[7]
Sources of Inspiration

Once you have printer's ink on your hands you will find that the ink sinks into your veins and gives you a new approach to type and the printed page. Everything concerned with print becomes of particular interest to you. This interest stretches well beyond books and magazines and newspapers and railway tickets. It concerns handwriting and maps and engraving and lithography and posters and the lettering on buildings and on tombstones. Any of these side-tracks may lead you towards some particular study and be your inspiration for years to come. You will find that the broad view of printing takes in many diverse subjects. For instance, if you begin to examine sixteenth- and seventeenth-century maps (Mercator, Saxton, Norden, Speed, Blaeu), you are sure to notice that the lettering bears a distinct resemblance to several italic types in present-day use (Blado, Centaur, Bembo). The map lettering, the best of which was engraved in Holland, and the types recut in the 1920s by the Monotype Corporation, have the same ancestry, namely the Chancery cursive handwriting from sixteenth-century Italy (Arrighi, Tagliente, Palatino, Cresci, Amphiareo).

The great maker and publisher of maps, Gerard Mercator, issued from Antwerp in 1540 a short treatise on map lettering. This was primarily intended as a guide for his own engravers. A *facsimile* was printed in 1930 by the Officina Bodoni and if you examine this reproduction you will see the resemblance to early sixteenth-century Italian writing and of course to italic types in use today, like Bembo.

If it is type design which becomes your special interest a fascinating history awaits your investigation. The few examples given at the end of Chapter 3 barely introduce the subject. Take a look at Updike's *Printing Types* listed at the end of this chapter. That book will demonstrate type design history and probably captivate your interest.

Decoration and illustration must be chosen and employed with skill. Decorative type units have already been mentioned, but drawings and engravings can also be used effectively with type. If you intend to create a style of your own, start by giving your press a name and also a device. Choose a name that looks well in type. For the mark choose something exceptionally well drawn or engraved and something which you will not grow tired of after seeing it many times on the printed page. There is no reason why you should not change the mark so long as the theme is continued. A number of different devices which I have used for the Miniature Press appear on several pages throughout this book. The sources are varied but the quality of the design unquestionable and they are related in theme. Above all avoid using anything for sentimental reasons. Particularly avoid asking a friend to draw you something if you may afterwards feel obliged to use it against your better judgment. The same warning applies to your own drawing; never use it unless it is unquestionably good. There are so many sources of excellent material that it is unforgivable to print anything second-rate. But if you use material from a printed source make sure that it is not in copyright, or, if it is still protected by copyright laws, ask for permission to use it.

Perhaps the most common source of inspiration springs from examining books and journals you meet and read in your everyday life. A personal list of inspirational material in this field appears at the end this chapter. Once you are interested in printing you naturally look more closely at books and periodicals and, if you have anything like a flair for typography, you may be able to say, just by taking a glance, at which press a book was printed. You will find yourself looking for the printer's imprint and often knowing it in advance of finding it. You will also see, in those books which are exceptionally well printed, a certain group of printers' names occurring over and over again. Your interest may rise considerably when, in following a particular printer's or publisher's work, you find a sudden marked change in style and relate this to a change in design staff of the firm in question. Changes in typographic style may sometimes be observed in one and the same designer. Perhaps the most startling case is to be found in Jan Tschichold's change from asymmetrical *sans serif* style of the Bauhaus period to his later traditional style. Typographical reactionaries ran riot after the first world war and such laws as were laid down by the Bauhaus have since been outmoded especially by their creators. The kind of text type then thought to be the most legible in principle has since been found unreadable in practice.

The following list of books and periodicals is a selection made from my personal library and does not pretend to be comprehensive. However, if you consult only a part of this small library, you will surely know what printing is about and even have some knowledge of design. These books and journals may well prove to be the inspiration you need for a lifetime of good printing.

BOOKS

Aldis, Harry G., *The Printed Book*, New Ed., 1947

Allen, L. M., *Printing with the Handpress*, 1969

Blumenthal, Joseph, *Art of the Printed Book*, 1974

Carter, Harry, *Fournier on Typefounding*, 1930

Cave, Roderick, *The Private Press*, 1971

Dibdin, T. F., *The Bibliographical Decameron*, 1817

Fairbank, Alfred, *A Book of Scripts*, 1945

Gill, Eric, *An Essay on Typography*, 2nd Ed., 1936

Harvey, Michael, *Lettering Design*, 1975

Holtzapfel, *Printing Apparatus for the Use of Amateurs*, New Ed., 1971

Jackson, Holbrook, *The Printing of Books*, 1938

Johnson, A. F., *One Hundred Title-Pages: 1500-1800*, 1938

Johnson, John, *Typographia*, 1824

McLean, Ruari, *Modern Book Design*, 1951

Moran, James, *Printing Presses*, 1973

Morison, Stanley, *John Fell*, 1967

Reed, Talbot Baines, *A History of the Old English Letter Foundries*, 2nd Ed., 1952

Simon, Oliver, *Introduction to Typography*, 1954

Simon & Carter, *Printing Explained*, 1931

Southward, John, *Practical Printing*, 4th Ed., 1892

Steinberg, Henry, *Five Hundred Years of Printing*, 1955

Updike, Daniel Berkley, *Printing Types*, 2nd Ed., 1937

Private Press Books [Ed. David Chambers], a description of new books and booklets, annually, 1960-

Journal of the Printing Historical Society [Ed. James Mosley and others], annually, 1965-

Graphis [Ed. Walter Herdeg], every two months, 1944-

Typographica [Ed. Herbert Spencer], 1949-67, 32 issues

Imprint [Ed. Gerard Meynell], began and finished in 1913, nine issues

Fleuron [Ed. Oliver Simon (I-IV) & Stanley Morison (V-VII)], 1923-30, seven issues

Typography [Ed. Robert Harling], 1936-39, eight issues

Alphabet & Image [Ed. Robert Harling], 1946-48, eight issues

Image [Ed. Robert Harling], 1949-52, eight issues

Signature [Ed. Oliver Simon], 1935-40, fifteen issues; New series, 1946-54, eighteen issues

Motif [Ed. Ruari McLean], 1958-64, thirteen issues

Woodcut used on the original proof of the first page of the Miniature Press's example for the Miniature Folio. It is a detail from a title-page printed at Toledo, 1554. The cut was later changed. See pages 123 and 133.

NUMBER 12   JUNE 1955

The Double Dolphin

A miniature newsletter well designed
and printed with care (and written
with the greatest economy of words)
might easily become a source of much
pleasure for the printer and his readers.
It could be a medium for information
or a testing-ground for new ideas in
verse or prose. The possibilities are
without limits but limits should be
imposed on the aims, on the style and
on the circulation. In other words,
first establish a purpose and then work
it out to the best of your ability from
a viewpoint embracing editorial and
typographic considerations.

Simple setting for a newsletter

[8]

The Little Presses

Bernard Newdigate wrote in the *London Mercury* about forty years ago: 'I hope my readers share my fondness for the work of the little presses,' and later, in *The Art of the Book* (London 1938): 'This account would be incomplete if no reference at all were made to the work of those gallant little presses which are worked as a hobby out of pure love for the craft of printing. . . .' There is little doubt that some privately owned presses have a good influence on printing in general.

The commercial standards in William Morris' time, with very few exceptions, were abominable. The fact that Morris' own work fell short of his ideals does not, in the long run, matter. He began a revival of interest in fine printing and, in a sense, paved the way for the Doves Press to 'attack the problem of Typography as presented by the ordinary book'. This problem was tackled with such skill that, when we now examine a page printed at the Doves Press (see page 47) we can still share in the delight which Cobden-Sanderson and Emery Walker must have felt on seeing the first proof. I will return to the Doves Press later. First I should like to enlarge on the need to 'attack' the problems of typography.

Dr Giovanni Mardersteig, director of a hand-press which, in its early days, employed types cast from the original matrices made by G. B. Bodoni, said in *The*

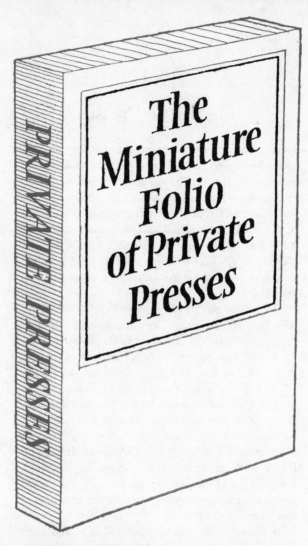

Hand-drawn lettering may sometimes provide a better solution to titling problems than can ever be achieved with type. This sketch by Michael Harvey shows how skilfully drawn letters may be employed.

Officina Bodoni (1929), 'The mere fact that the hand-press is an ideal instrument for experiment is of incalculable value. Without experiment, without the constant examination of all the given possibilities, the perfect solution of a typographic problem can never be obtained.' In 1938 the first number of a journal called *Typography* was issued by the Shenval Press with the following message from Stanley Morison: 'Typography today does not so much need inspiration or revival as investigation.' Whether we call this 'attacking the problems' or 'examining the possibilities' or 'investigation' it is one and the same thing. It is the little presses which are most suited to work in this field of research.

The existence of private presses goes back at least to 1581 – some authorities say back as far as the end of the fifteenth century. Early presses were founded for private use either because of the scarcity of printers or because of the religious or political control of printing. For instance, Edmund Campion, a Catholic Father, owned a press at Stonor, near Henley-on-Thames, in 1581. He had 400 copies of *Decem Rationes* printed and distributed. No commercial printer would have undertaken the work which, at that time, was considered seditious and although Campion was later arrested and beheaded at the Tower of London he had achieved, through his own press, what would otherwise have been impossible. Another early press was set up in 1584 by the astronomer Tycho Brahe who lived in the castle of Uranienborg, an island between Sweden and Denmark. This press he established to publish his own researches. On the island he also had bookbinders and a paper-mill and to the island he invited artists to make the illustrations he required in his books of astronomy. But this press which began with such a high potential proved to be shortlived – unlike another specially situated workshop, the Stanbrook Abbey Press, which was founded in 1876 and now flourishes under the capable and inspired hand of Hildelith Cumming, Sister of the enclosed Benedictine Order. At Greenwich, *c*. 1554, Conrade Freeman printed privately, as did Sir Henry Savile at Eton in 1607. Several eighteenth-century presses are recorded including the following:

Peter Whitfield, Liverpool, 1749
Raglan Castle, Monmouthshire, 1750
Strawberry Hill Press, Twickenham, 1757-89
Mme de Pompadour, Versailles, *c*. 1760
John Wilkes, Westminster, 1763
Glynde Press, nr Lewes, *c*. 1770
Benjamin Franklin, Passy, 1776-85
R. Greene, Lichfield, *c*. 1776

Of these the Strawberry Hill Press, which was owned by Sir Horace Walpole, is the best known. John Wilkes printed (or caused to be printed) privately an obscene *Essay on Woman* which earned him expulsion from the House of Commons. Benjamin Franklin, printer and American ambassador, set up a private press at Passy (now a suburb of Paris) partly for printing official documents and partly to produce 'bagatelles' for the amusement of his friends. *The Blank Passport*, which Franklin printed in 1781, employed script types specially cut by Pierre-Simon Fournier.

At the turn of the century William Davy, a Devonshire parson, finding errors in the first edition of his *System of Divinity*, asked for a new edition to be printed.

His publisher refused and Davy purchased a press, type and paper. He harnessed his gardener to the press and apprenticed his housemaid to the type-setting. After twelve years' work, a new edition of fourteen sets each of twenty-six volumes was issued – which surely indicates that, when typomania is coupled with religious fervour, anything up to a miracle may be achieved.

Early in the nineteenth century two private presses appeared somewhat in keeping with Sir Horace Walpole's and certainly progenitors of the presses which followed at the end of the century. In 1813 Sir Egerton Brydges established his Lee Priory Press near Canterbury. He employed two printers, John Johnson and John Warwick. Johnson left the press in 1817, six years before it closed, and wrote his *Typographia* (*or the Printers' Instructor*) which was published in 1824. In 1815 Alexander Boswell, the son of James Boswell, established his Auchinleck Press in Dumfriesshire and maintained it until 1818.

Private printing has sometimes begun almost by accident. There are accounts of people who, as it were, stumbled upon the notion that it would be amusing to own some equipment and print. For instance Charles Hulbert of Shrewsbury wrote, printed and published four books (in all, about 700 pages) between 1842 and 1857. Will Ransom says of Hulbert: 'According to his own story he strolled into an auction room in an idle moment and found a printing press being sold. He bought it and thenceforward devoted himself to authorship and typography.'

During the middle of the nineteenth century one very important press was established by a boy, nine or ten years of age. This was the Daniel Press. Charles

THE FOUNDING OF SOME PRIVATE PRESSES

PRESS	DATE	DIRECTOR	LOCATION	TYPE
Uranienborg	1584	*Tycho Brahe*	Denmark	
Strawberry Hill	1757	*Horace Walpole*	Twickenham	*Caslon*
Daniel	1845	*Dr Charles Daniel*	Frome	*(Fell)*
Mosher	1891	*Thomas Bird Mosher*	Portland, Maine	*Caslon*
Kelmscott	1891	*William Morris*	Hammersmith	*Golden, Troy, Chaucer*
Eragny	1894	*L. & E. Pissarro*	Epping	*Brook*
Ashendene	1894	*C. H. St J. Hornby*	Chelsea	*Subiaco, Ptolemy*
Vale	1896	*Charles Ricketts*	Strand, London	*Vale, Avon, King's*
Essex House	1898	*C. R. Ashbee*	Mile End, London	*Endeavour, Prayer Book*
Doves	1900	*C–S & E. W.*	Hammersmith	*Doves*
Village	1903	*F. & B. Goudy*	Park Ridge, Illinois	*Village*
Cranach	1913	*Count Kessler*	Weimar	*Janson Antiqua*
Dard Hunter	1915	*Dard Hunter*	Ohio	*Hunter*
Romney Street	1915	*Francis Meynell*	Westminster	*Fell*
Grabhorn	1919	*E. & R. Grabhorn*	San Francisco	*Goudy (various)*
Golden Cockerel	1921	*Harold M. Taylor*	Waltham St Lawrence	*Golden Cockerel, Caslon*
Gregynog	1922	*R. A. Maynard*	Newtown, Montgomeryshire	*Kennerley*
Bodoni	1922	*Dr G. Mardersteig*	Montagnola di Lugano	*Bodoni (original types)*
Nonesuch	1923	*Francis Meynell*	Bloomsbury	*Fell, Janson etc.*

Daniel printed letter by letter from types held in his hands and inked with a smudge from his thumb. Naturally his alignment was approximate but this enthusiasm was rewarded when his father bought him a toy press. This press may have been a Parlour press (see page 29) which was first manufactured at that time. The young printer thanked his father with a letter which is of particular interest since it shows that, from this early age, Daniel was sensitive to the appearance of a printed page. Part of the letter runs: 'please do not mind my very bad printing, for when any one looks on any part of it, it is really immensely, terribly, and dreadfully horrible.' The Daniel Press flourished at Frome from 1845 to 1863. In 1850 an Albion press was bought and in 1874 the equipment was moved to Oxford where Daniel used it until 1906. He printed numerous first editions of Robert Bridges.

Then, in 1876, an event occurred for which the Daniel Press will always be remembered. Dr Daniel, with the co-operation of Professor Bartholomew Price, discovered the Fell types and matrices which had lain out of use at the Oxford University Press for 150 years. Dr John Fell, Bishop of Oxford, had secured punches, matrices and a type-founder from Holland in 1666 and established a foundry for the Press which was set up in the Sheldonian Theatre in 1669. With permission Daniel used these types for his own printing. Such revivals as this are of the greatest importance and it should be noted that one of the famous English type-faces, Caslon Old Face, had been revived some twenty years earlier by Charles Whittingham of the Chiswick Press and William Pickering. The foundry, then belonging to Henry Caslon, had to be searched to find

This wood-engraving by John Petts is from Susanna and the Elders, *hand-printed by Jonah Jones and privately issued from the Caseg Press in 1948. Petts later became a maker of stained glass windows and Jones became a sculptor.*

the punches and matrices of this face.

A little press which flourished for a bare three years whilst Daniel was a boy at Frome, and which printed purely for pleasure, was the Roehampton Press. Here, a few miles from London, Jane Frances Bickersteth – assisted by Sir Anthony Panizzi (chief librarian of the

British Museum) – printed a number of single leaf periodicals which she sold for one farthing each. Jane was about twelve years old when she began to print in 1848, and the bibliography of her press is a simple one:

I. THE ELF, 31 *numbers*, 1848

II. THE FAIRY, 18 *numbers*, 1849

III. THE MITE, 78 *numbers*, 1850-51

Of some of these numbers only two or three copies were printed.

Another purely-for-pleasure press was the Rochester Press, run by Edwin Roffe from 1858 to 1876. Roffe was by trade a steel engraver and he built his own press employing a simple carpenter's handscrew for the action. Fourteen publications are recorded by Will Ransom (in his *Private Presses and their Books*, 1929) and the average number of copies of each item is about twenty. In 1861 Roffe declared his affections in a few lines of simple verse:

> I must confess,
> I love my press;
> For when I print,
> I know no stint
>   of joy.

Whilst the Daniel Press flourished at Oxford, William Morris began to print at Hammersmith and Thomas Bird Mosher established his press at Portland, Maine, during the same year, 1891. Daniel and Mosher were not great printers like Morris but they used excellent types and their books are typographically simple. Morris, on the other hand, designed his own types and filled his pages with so much decoration that, as McMurtrie says in *The Book: the story of printing &*

Woodcut illustration by Robert Wyss for Heloise and Abelard,
Kim Taylor and the Ark Press, 1973

bookmaking (1937), 'even if one endeavours to read them, the mind is distracted from the sense of the author by spots or masses of decoration so insistent in area and color as to completely overshadow the text'. Updike, whose criticisms are generous, says in *Printing Types* (1937), 'As we look at Morris's typographical achievements in perspective, they seem to be more those of a decorator applying his decorative talents to printing, than the work of a printer . . . He did not make books that it was a pleasure to read. If Morris admired Jenson's fonts, it is hard to see why he did not copy their best points more closely.' Nevertheless after Morris came a succession of important presses and it is certain that the influence of his Kelmscott Press was both wide and valuable. But whether the influence of Sir Emery Walker was wider and more valuable it is difficult to say. Sir Emery gave advice to Morris as he did to the Ashendene Press, to Count Kessler and to Cobden-Sanderson with whom he set up the Doves Press in 1900.

The Doves Press achieved what Morris talked about. It made fine books that were easy (and therefore a pleasure) to read. After the heavily decorated works from the Kelmscott, Eragny, Vale and Essex House presses, the absence of decoration is all the more remarkable in Doves books. The Doves type was based on Nicolas Jenson's roman letter and it has been said that Sir Emery 'translated' the type of Jenson's *Pliny* (printed in 1476), had the drawings made under his personal supervision, arranged for the punches to be cut by Edward Prince and the matrices to be struck at the Scottish typefoundry of Miller & Richard.

The Doves type was perhaps the most important

private press face of the period and the story of its disappearance is of some interest. A few years after the press was founded a quarrel developed over the possession of the type and Emery Walker withdrew from the partnership. In 1909 a legal agreement was drawn up between Emery Walker and Cobden-Sanderson under which the Doves material was to remain in C-S's hands but was finally to belong to whichever man survived the other. However, nine years before his death, C-S began the destruction of the Doves material by throwing punches and matrices into the Thames at Hammersmith. At this time no one knew what was going on but by 1917 C-S had become so used to the practice that he perhaps could see no wrong in it His obsession was such that he had identified himself with the type and was determined never to let it fall into the hands of E.W. He wrote, in a letter to Sydney Cockerell dated 9 September 1917, '. . . alone and with only all the stars of heaven to witness, night after night, I committed the type and the punches to the bed of the River Thames. . . .'

E.W., on discovering that the material (which legally was his) had been destroyed by his former friend and partner, contemplated having a new set of punches cut. Unfortunately Edward Prince died before this could be accomplished and nothing at all is known to survive.

In both American and English fine printing the name of Bruce Rogers appears constantly since the 1890's. At least one of Thomas Bird Mosher's early title-pages was lettered by B.R. (as he was usually styled) and towards the end of 1916 Bruce Rogers came to England. With Emery Walker and Wilfred Merton he founded the Mall Press at Hammersmith in 1917 and printed

Dürer's *Of the Just Shaping of Letters*, a folio edition in Centaur type for the Grolier Club, New York. That same year B.R. was invited by the Syndics to make a report on the typography of the then Cambridge University Press. Three years later, in Cambridge, Mass., Bruce Rogers began his sixteen years' term as printing adviser to the Harvard University Press and, at the same time, he was collaborating with the printer Will Rudge. B.R.'s remarkably ingenious arrangements of type ornaments were an inspiration to many designers and printers and in Rudge's office he used a miniature type-case filled with different fleurons. With the aid of an ink-pad B.R. evolved trial designs, combining the rough hand-made prints of the ornaments with his drawn *layouts*. To such layouts he would sometimes add the following *colophon*:

Painfully printed
at the Sign of the Sore Thumb

Quite a number of private printers have become famous for the literary value of their books rather than for the manner in which they were printed. Several works by R. L. Stevenson were privately printed in Switzerland under the imprint 'S. L. Osbourne & Co.', 1881-2. In 1902 the Misses Elizabeth and Lily Yeats started the Dun Emer Press which later changed its name to the Cuala Press. Most of the work published was by W. B. Yeats, but they also printed George Russell, J. M. Synge, Tagore and Ezra Pound. Sir

Francis Meynell's first and purely private Romney Street Press began in 1915 and printed by hand *Ten Poems, 1913-15* by Alice Meynell. Two years later Leonard and Virginia Woolf bought a small press, some Caslon type and a manual of instructions and began to print at their home in Richmond upon Thames. First they produced and published two stories written by themselves under the Hogarth Press imprint. Then came *Prelude* by Katherine Mansfield; *Poems* by T. S. Eliot; *Kew Gardens* by Virginia Woolf; *Story of the Siren* by E. M. Forster, and *Paris* by Hope Mirrless. After excellent reviews in *The Times Literary Supplement* success as publishers came to the Woolfs so quickly that, within three years, they had ceased to print and had established themselves as publishers. For three years (1919-21) John Rodker printed, at his Ovid Press in Hampstead, literary works including both T. S. Eliot and Ezra Pound. At Paris in 1923 the Three Mountains Press began and printed during its five years' existence, works by Ernest Hemingway and Ezra Pound. Laura Riding and Robert Graves printed their own work at the Seizin Press which they began in 1928. Most items from these 'literary' presses have become collectors' pieces and it is not at all uncommon to find that a few leaves of poetry printed by one of them and sold originally for a shilling now fetch rare book prices at auction.

One of these little presses developed into a publishing office which became equally well known for its standard of scholarship and for the typographical excellence of its books. Sir Francis Meynell called this venture (begun in 1923) the Nonesuch Press and he published many fine books at modest prices.

The Three
Admirable Accidents of

ANDREA de PIERO

FROM THE FIRST ENGLYSHED
EDITION OF THE DECAMERON
OF JOHN BOCCACCIO WITH
WOODCUTS BY

MCMLIV
At the Gravesend Press
LEXINGTON, KENTUCKY

Joseph Graves, proprietor of the Gravesend Press, earned a living by running a clothing store. He also enjoyed cooperation and friendship from Fritz Kredel, Caroline and Victor Hammer and R. Hunter Middleton, Chicago's printer and collector of the work of Thomas Bewick. Graves was a remarkably fine printer.

The Flying Fame, which was founded by Claud Lovat Fraser, Ralph Hodgson and Holbrook Jackson, was a press defying any kind of pigeon-holing. It flourished for less than two years during 1912 and 1913. Nevertheless it succeeded in producing ninety-one small items. The Flying Fame was an excellent example of printing for pleasure. Holbrook Jackson describes the formation of the press in his essay on Fraser published in the first issue of *The Fleuron* (1923): 'The idea was the outcome of much playful talk, banter and sketching and squib-writing by a group of writers and a painter or so who used to meet for coffee in the smoking room of a Strand teashop during 1912.' The three founders of the press each put down £5 for equipment and the enterprise began. Lovat Fraser did most of the printing and designing which followed the chap-book style. The crude drawing and typography were both quaint and attractive.

Sometimes a private press has been a starting point of the professional printer or typographer. The Perpetua Press of David Bland and Vivian Ridler is an example. This press existed between 1934 and 1937, and, opposite, I have reproduced one of Lotte Reiniger's silhouettes from Eric White's *The Little Chimney Sweep*, printed in 1936. When the press closed in the following year David Bland joined the production office of Faber & Faber, and Vivian Ridler joined the University Press, Oxford, where he has for many years been Printer to the University. He has since revived the Perpetua Press at his home for the production of occasional pieces.

A press with a resident artist is unusual but it happens to be the case at Stanbrook Abbey, where Sister

Silhouette by Lotte Reiniger from Eric White's
The Little Chimney Sweep *printed at the*
Perpetua Press, Bristol, 1936

Meinrad Craighead is in the same monastery as Sister
Hildelith Cumming. However, many small presses are
associated with artists. In New Jersey, Joseph Low,
whilst designing and drawing commercially, also prints
and issues work from his private Quattrocchi Press,
later renamed Eden Hill Press. The Ark Press, founded
at St Ives, Cornwall, by Kim Taylor in 1954, when the
first edition of this little book was being written, has a
distinguished association with contemporary artists including Ben Shahn, Robert Wyss, Felix Hoffmann,
Cyril Satorsky and Otto Rohse. Eric Gill was associated
with several presses beginning with the St Dominic's
Press and including Cranach, Ashendene, Golden
Cockerel and Hague & Gill. Reynolds Stone with his
international reputation as an engraver, is quite un-

known as a private printer, yet he has a remarkable collection of hand-presses (see *Journal of the Printing Historical Society*, No. 2). Fritz Kredel, during his later years in America, was associated with Joseph Graves' Gravesend Press at Lexington, Kentucky. Giovanni Mardersteig on his hand-press at Verona has printed the work of a great many artists, including Reynolds Stone and Fritz Kredel.

Mardersteig's press, established at Montagnola in 1922 and in operation since 1927 at Verona, is beyond doubt the most important private press. The Officina Bodoni was so named by Giovanni Mardersteig in 1922, because he began printing with original Bodoni types. Since then he has used many others and distinguished himself and the Press by designing three text types, Griffo, Zeno and Dante. The scholarship, design and printing of books from this press combine to make it the most important Officina. Mardersteig's researches concerning Felice Feliciano and the revival of inscribed Roman letters in fifteenth-century Verona, concerning uncut, unpublished designs for woodcuts of Dürer, concerning the identity of the fifteenth-century artist, Liberale da Verona, of *Aesop's Fables*, Verona 1479, concerning the little known alphabet of Francesco Torniello, published in 1517, these are all works of scholarship which have been published from Mardersteig's Officina in quite superlative books.

[9]
Where to Buy Your Equipment

In the twenty years since *Printing for Pleasure* was first published changes have taken place in the printing world. It is not just that the industry has gone metric but particularly that lithographic printing now dominates letterpress printing and that the *collotype* process has virtually disappeared. In contemporary printing the computer works almost exclusively in the realm of filmsetting and the casting of hot metal types is soon to become a process of historic importance rather than daily use.

Effects of change and inflation go against the setting up of a small press; for instance, the diminishing number of suppliers of accessories and the collecting of early iron presses as antiques at high prices, the disappearance of the smaller paper mills, standardization of paper-making and the economic difficulties of importing typographical material.

Despite all this evidence on the negative side the miniature workshop for experimental letterpress printing – which is my view of a private press – will survive and can be established today. At the end of the present chapter are included a number of suppliers who, according to latest information, are active still. However, the would-be-printer has several sources of information open to him or her.

1. Write for catalogues to any of the suppliers listed below.

2. Always keep an eye on *Industrial Exchange and Mart* (published in the U.K. every Monday) when you know what sort of equipment you want.

3. Write to the British Printing Society, BM/ISPA, London WC1 for full details of their Society whose objects are: (i) to unite full-time, part-time and hobby printers in friendly association; (ii) to improve the standard of craftsmanship of its members in printing and allied crafts; (iii) to encourage printing as a hobby.

4. You can buy copies of *Private Press Books* (published annually by the Private Libraries Association and edited by David Chambers at Ravelston, South View Road, Pinner, Middlesex), which is a checklist of books and leaflets issued during the previous year from private presses throughout the world. From this list you can discover who are your nearest printing neighbours, what presses they use, what sort of work they do, which types and papers they use. Some of them like to correspond with the owners of other presses; but see that you have something to offer, even if it is only a good letter, before attempting to disturb your neighbour who may well prefer to spend his time printing. Two important newsletters are issued in America (addresses on page 120): *Fine Print* (San Francisco) and *Bibliography Newsletter* (New York). Each includes items of interest to the bibliophile on both sides of the Atlantic – publishing projects, exhibitions, international meetings, etc.

5. Consult *Printing Trades Directory* for suppliers of presses, type, paper, blocks, ink and accessories in the U.K.

6. Consult *Yellow Pages* (*Pink Pages* in Australia) under Paper Merchants, Printers Services, Printers Supplies, Printing Ink Manufacturers, Printing Machine Manufacturers, Process Engraving. Because this source is up-to-date and regional on a world-wide basis it is (together with *Private Press Books*) certainly of importance. Not all trade suppliers are keen to take small orders from private presses but you will soon learn who, in your district, is sympathetic.

7. Ask at the offices of your local library or museum and enquire if there are any special collections of books available to you; or if there are any societies, like the Imprint Society of Newcastle, to which you could belong. The special library of books on printing and allied subjects at the St Bride Institute, Fleet Street, London may be of value to you and, housed in the same building, is a small museum of printing presses. There are, of course, some presses to be seen in the Science Museum, South Kensington, London.

SOURCES OF MATERIALS

The list of names and addresses of suppliers (overleaf) has been compiled from letters of recommendation by private printers throughout the world. It is anything but complete and the use of other aids mentioned at the beginning of this chapter will be necessary to find sources of supply in many countries and districts.

Adana (Printing Machines) Ltd,
15 Church Street, Twickenham, Middlesex
Presses, type, supplies

Excelsior Printers Supply Co. Ltd,
City-Gate Unit, Nobel Road, Ely Industrial Estate,
Angel Road, London N18   *Presses, supplies*

Stephenson Blake, Caslon Letter Foundry,
Sheffield
(also see under Mouldtype)   *Presses, type, supplies*

Yendall & Co. Ltd,
Riscatype House, Red Lion Court,
Fleet Street, London EC4   *Type*

Mouldtype Foundry Ltd,
50 Farringdon Street, London EC4
(agent for Caslon Letter Foundry)   *Type*

Grosvenor Chater & Co. Ltd,
Laycock Street, London N1   *Paper*

Frank Grunfield Ltd,
32 Bedford Square, London WC1   *Paper*

SWITZERLAND/ZURICH
Dr E. Blatter & Co.,
Ecke Staubstrasse 1/Seestrasse, 8038, Zürich
Presses, type, supplies

U.S.A./ILLINOIS
Castcraft Printing Supply Inc.,
1100 South Kostner Ave, Chicago, Ill. 60623   *Type*

Graphic Arts Equipment Co.,
1260 S. Wabash Ave, Chicago, Ill. 60605
Presses, supplies

U.S.A./EAST COAST
Andrews/Nelson/Whitehead,
31-10 48th Avenue, Long Island City, NY 11101
Paper

N.Y. Central Supply Co.,
62 Third Avenue, New York, NY 10003
Paper

Van Son Holland Ink Corp.,
Union & Liberty, Mineola, NY 11501
Ink

The Kelsey Company,
30 Cross Street, Meriden, CT 06450
Presses, supplies

Out-of-Sorts Foundry,
25 Old Colony Drive, Larchmont, NY 10538
Type

Turnbaugh Printers Supply Co.,
104 Sporting Hill Road, Mechanicsburg, PA 17055
Presses, type, supplies

Mike Carbone,
2031 Federal Street, Camden, NJ 08105
Presses, supplies

U.S.A./WEST
Los Angeles Typefounders Inc.,
225 East Pico Blvd, Los Angeles, CA 90015
Type

The Printers' Shop,
4047 Transport Street, Palo Alto, CA 94303
Presses, type, supplies

Griffin Brothers, Western Inc.,
365 Brannam Place, San Francisco, CA 94103
Type, supplies

Somerset Equipment Co.,
1261 Howard Street, San Francisco, CA 94103
Presses, supplies

CANADA/ONTARIO
Don Black Linecasting Service,
117 Phyllis Street, Scarborough, Toronto, Ont. MIM IY2
Type, supplies and, occasionally, small presses

Sydney R. Stone Ltd,
6 Lisgar Street, Toronto, Ont. M6J 3G2
Presses, supplies

Buntin Reid Paper Co. Ltd,
800 King Street West, Toronto, Ont. M5V IPI
Paper (branch in Montreal)

Kruger Fine Papers,
793 Pharmacy Road, Toronto, Ont. MIL 3K3
Paper and binding cloth (branch in Montreal)

Inter City Papers Ltd,
560 Hensall Circle, Mississauga, Ont. L5A IYI
Supplies

AUSTRALIA/VICTORIA
B. J. Ball,
63 River Street, Richmond, Melbourne, Vic. 3121
Presses and supplies
Catalogue on request, branches in all States (see also *Pink Pages*)

Sidney Cooke,
3 Millers Road, Brooklyn, Melbourne, Vic. 3025   *Inks*

Dudley E. King,
Williams Street, Melbourne, Vic. 3000   *Monotype setting*

118

AUSTRALIA/NEW SOUTH WALES
Dolphin & Hannan Pty Ltd,
29 Parramatta Road, Sydney 2000   *Supplies*

F. T. Wimble & Co. Ltd,
11 South Street, Rydelmore, Sydney 2116   *Supplies*

AUSTRALIA/QUEENSLAND
F. T. Wimble & Co. Ltd,
17 Halford Street, Newstead, Brisbane 4000   *Supplies*

AUSTRALIA/WEST AUSTRALIA
F. T. Wimble & Co. Ltd,
339 Newcastle Street, Perth 6000   *Supplies*

AUSTRALIA/SOUTH AUSTRALIA
F. T. Wimble & Co. Ltd,
246 Franklin Street, Adelaide 5000   *Supplies*

NEW ZEALAND/AUCKLAND
Morrison Printing Inks and Machinery Ltd,
Wall Road, Penrose, Auckland 6   *Supplies*

F. T. Wimble & Co., N.Z. Ltd,
Dryden Place, Ellerslie, Auckland 6   *Supplies*
(*branches in Wellington, Christchurch and Dunedin*)

R.S.A./JOHANNESBURG
Cawse & Malcolm (Pty) Ltd,
P.O. Box 6342, Johannesburg
Agent for Adana (*Printing Machines*) *Ltd*

WEST AFRICA/NIGERIA
Wiggins Teape (West Africa) Ltd,
P.O. Box 95, 23 Burma Road, Apapa, Nigeria
Agent for Adana (*Printing Machines*) *Ltd*

JAPAN/TOKYO
Toyo Koeki Co. Ltd,
Dainisanko Building, 2nd Floor, 12 Akefune Cho,
Shiba-Nishikubo, Minato-Ku, Tokyo, Japan
Agent for Adana (*Printing Machines*) *Ltd*

You may wish to start a personal library of finely printed books and of books concerning printing and bibliography and allied subjects like typefounding, paper-making, type design, book illustration, graphic art and lettering design. The bookshops listed below issue catalogues and always stock books on some of these subjects.

Bertram Rota Ltd,
4 Savile Row,
London W1

Erasmus Antiquariat,
Spui 2,
Amsterdam, Holland

Tony Appleton,
28 Florence Road,
Brighton,
Sussex

Dawson's Bookshop,
535 N. Larchmont Blvd,
Los Angeles,
Calif. 90004, U.S.A.

Keith Hogg,
82 High Street,
Tenterden,
Kent

Chiswick Bookshop,
Walnut Tree Hill Road,
Sandy Hook,
Conn. 06482, U.S.A.

SOURCES OF NEWSLETTERS

Fine Print Write for subscription details to PO Box 7741, San Francisco, Calif. 94120

Bibliography Newsletter Write to Professor Terry Belanger, 21 Claremont Avenue, New York, NY, 10027

TYPE SPECIMEN BOOKS

Type for Books Printed by Mackays of Chatham and available from The Bodley Head.

Book Types Printed by Clowes and available from them at 15 Cavendish Square, London W1

Glossary

A list of printing terms used in this book together with some others in common use. The page numbers in parentheses following each entry refer to the first use of the word in this book.

AMPERSAND, short version of 'and' derived from 'et': &, &, &.

ARABIC FIGURES (derived from Arabic writing). Old style or hanging: 1 2 3 4 5; modern or lining: 1 2 3 4 5.

ASCENDERS, strokes of lower-case letters which project above the x-height, as b d h, etc. (32)

ASTERISK, star-shaped reference mark.

BACK, in a book page, the inner margin between the type and the spine.

BACKING-UP, to print the reverse side of a sheet when one side is already printed. (26)

BEARD, the distance from the face of the type to the front or back (bevel plus shoulder = beard). At the side, the space is called side-bearing.

BED, flat surface of a press on which the forme rests. (22)

BEVEL, the metal which slopes from the face to the shoulder of a type. (33)

BLACK LETTER, general term for typefaces based on mediaeval script. Also called Gothic, or Old English Text.

BLOCK, type-high printing surface of lino, wood, zinc or copper, cut or engraved (either by hand or by photo-chemical methods). (17)

BODY, the shank of a piece of type. (32)

BOOKPLATE, a printed label of ownership pasted on the inside front cover of a book. (24)

BROADSHEET, a sheet of unfolded paper printed on one side only. (17)

CAPITALS, upper-case letters, A B C. (32)

CAPTION, description or legend usually placed beneath illustration. (81)

CARD FOUNT, the smallest complete fount of type stocked and sold by a typefounder. (36)

CARTRIDGE PAPER, a tough kind of paper made with a rough or smooth surface and used for printing or for drawing. (86)

CASE, a tray divided into compartments to hold type and spaces. (35)

CEREMONIAL OPENING, the beginning of a text or chapter which starts with large initial letter.

CHASE, a metal frame into which type, blocks, etc. are fixed before being printed. (22)

CLUMPS, metal line-spacing material of 6 pts thickness or more. (58)

COLLOTYPE, a photographic process of reproduction for making facsimiles using gelatine-based plates. (113)

COLOPHON, a note or the finishing stroke in a book usually found on the final leaf and giving details of the author, printer, date and place where printed.

COMPOSING, see SETTING. (13)

COMPOSING STICK, adjustable metal tray into which lines of type may be set and justified. (58)

COUNTER, in type, a depression enclosed or partly enclosed by the printing surface, as the centre of an O. (33)

COUNTER-PUNCH, tool used in the making of a punch.

DABBER, a sheepskin- or buckskin-covered pad on a wooden handle used to ink type. Also called an inkball. (69)

DESCENDERS, strokes of lower-case letters which project below the x-height, as g j p. Also called extruders. (32)

DEVICE, a trademark or design introduced by a printer or publisher on the title-page or at the end of the text to distinguish his productions. (60)

A device for the Miniature Press, from John Speed's map of Rutland engraved in Holland in 1610. It was used on the first and last pages of the Miniature Folio of Private Presses (see pages 133-136) and replaced the device shown on page 93.

DISS, see DISTRIBUTION.

DISTRIBUTION, the returning of type to its proper compartment in the typecase after printing. (67)

EM, the square of any type size. The 12 pts em (pica) is a standard unit for measuring print. (35)

EM QUADRAT, a square unit of spacing material. The pica em quad = 12 pts × 12 pts. (35)

EN, unit of space equal to half an em. (35)

ENGRAVING, drawing or lettering cut into wood or metal and used as a printing plate. The metal plates were intaglio and copper but gave way to steel about 1830.

EXTRUDERS, name for ascenders and descenders. (32)

FACE, the printing surface of a type. Also refers to the design of a fount. (16)

FACSIMILE, an exact copy; a faithful reproduction in the size of the original. (89)

FLATBED, a press which has the printing forme on a plain surface, as distinct from a curved one, and is usually horizontal. (30)

FLEURON, a printer's ornament, originally flower-shaped, cast as a printing type. (42)

FOOT, part of a type. Also margin at bottom of book page. (34)

FORME, type, furniture etc. locked in a chase ready for printing. (22)

FOUNT, a complete set of type characters of one particular size and face made up to a specified weight or number of characters. (14)

FRISKET, iron frame on an Albion press, or strips of metal (grippers) on a platen press, for holding a sheet of paper in the correct position whilst it is being printed and for pulling the paper away from the type after the impression has been made. (22)

FURNITURE, pieces of wood or metal used in the make-up of a forme where margins and other white spaces are required. (57)

GROOVE, a channel cut in the base of a piece of type thus giving it two feet to stand on. (34)

HAIR SPACE, thin piece of metal used for spacing type. They are available in brass (1 pt in thickness) and in copper ($\frac{1}{2}$ pt in thickness). (35)

HALF-TONE BLOCK, a photo-engraved printing plate (usually of copper) which reproduces tone values by means of a screen of dots varying in size. (77)

HEIGHT-TO-PAPER, 0.918 of an inch, the standard height of type in England and America. (33)

IMPOSITION, the arrangement of pages which are to be printed together so that correct sequence is obtained when the printed sheet is folded; also of the position of the type on the page. (24)

IMPRESSION, the pressure applied to a forme of type by the cylinder or platen. (17)

IMPRINT, the name and address of the printer, appearing in books etc. as required by Law.

INFERIOR, a special sort cast on the body so that it prints below the base line of lower-case letters, viz: m_2, m_3.

INITIAL LETTER, a large capital letter, plain or decorated, used at the beginning of a text or chapter or as a decoration.

INKBALL, see DABBER.

INTERLEAVE, to place sheets of tissue between the printed sheets as they are taken from the press. (76)

ITALIC, the lower-case fount introduced by Aldus Manutius at the beginning of the sixteenth century based on the Chancery hand, usually sloped, *a b c d e f*. Sloped capitals appeared later. (8)

JUSTIFY, to set lines of type in the composing stick to an exact measure. (83)

KERN, any part of the face of a type which overhangs its body. (32)

LAID SURFACE, of paper which shows parallel wire-marks of the mould in which it is made. (86)

LAYOUT, the preparation of copy for setting indicating the position of type and/or illustrations on the page.

LEADERS, a row of dots to lead the eye from one point to another on the page; a poor practice.

LEADING, the spacing between lines of type. This may be done with strips of lead, wood or plastic. (38)

LEADS, line-spacing material of less than 6 pts thickness. (32)

LEAF, in a book, a single sheet or two pages.

LETTERPRESS, the process of printing from type and blocks cut or etched in relief. (77)

LETTER-SPACING, the insertion of spaces between the letters of a word. (66)

LIGATURES, in the strictest sense *ſt* and *et* but generally applied to tied letters such as ffl where two or more letters are cast on one body. (36)

LINE BLOCK, a printing surface, usually of zinc, made photo-chemically to reproduce in line as opposed to half-tone (*q.v.*). (60)

LITHOGRAPHY, the process of printing from a flat stone (nowadays zinc) surface treated by hand or by photography so that only the areas required to print pick up ink. The rest of the plate remains ink-repellent.

LOWER-CASE, the alphabet of miniscules, a b c d. (32)

LYE, an alkaline preparation for cleaning type after use. (58)

MAKE-READY, preparation of the forme (see overlay and underlay). (73)

MATRIX, in typefounding, a mould from which a type is cast. (31)

MECHANICAL TINT, a tint applied by the engraver to a line block to vary tone and texture. (85)

MITRE BLOCK, tool used to make right-angle or diagonal cuts in wood. (58)

MUTTON, popular name for em quad. (35)

NICK, groove on the front of a type-body. (32)

NUT, popular name for en quad. (35)

OPENING, the two facing pages of a book or leaflet.

OVERLAY, part of the process of make-ready whereby packing is fixed to the platen of the press. (73)

PAGE, one side of a leaf of paper. In a book the right-hand side is called recto and the left-hand side verso. (13)

PAGINATION, the numbering of pages in a book.

PHOTO-ENGRAVING, the preparation of a relief printing surface on a plate by one of several methods employing photographic, chemical and mechanical means. (85)

PICA, a measurement of 12 pts.

PIN-MARK, a round depression in the side of the shank of a type made by the pin which ejects the type from the mould. (33)

PLANING, process by which the types are pressed into their correct seating. (65)

PLATEN, the flat surface of a printing machine which presses a sheet of paper against the type. (17)

PLATEN PACKING, sheets of paper covering the platen used to adjust the pressure of the paper against the inked type forme. (71)

POINT SYSTEM, standard of typographical measurement (72 pts=approx. 1 inch) employed in England and America. (32)

PRESS-POINTS, spikes fixed on the tympan of an Albion or similar press as a means of making register between two or more impressions on a single sheet. (26)

PROCESS-ENGRAVING, any of several photo-mechanical methods of producing relief blocks or plates for printing illustrations. (73) *see also* PHOTO-ENGRAVING

PROGRESSION PROOFS, a first proof marked with corrections and subsequent proofs marked and corrected again until a CLEAN PROOF (one requiring no corrections) is achieved. (80)

PROOF, a trial print from type, blocks or plates. (26)

PUNCH, the engraved character on steel which is to be struck into copper to form a matrix for type-founding (see illustration on page 42). (31)

QUADRATS (QUADS), metal spacing material smaller than 24 pts square. (35)

QUOINS, wedges of wood or metal, or mechanically expanding blocks, used to lock up type in a forme. (58)

QUOTATIONS, metal spacing material of 24 pts square and larger. The casting is usually hollow. (35)

RECTO, a right-hand page normally folioed with odd numbers. The topside of a leaf (see VERSO).

REGLET, line spacing material of wood from $1\frac{1}{2}$-18 pts in thickness. Also available in plastic. (36)

RIDERS, rollers which ride on the backs of other rollers to aid the distribution of ink. (69)

ROLLER, a cylindrical instrument used to transfer ink from a plate to the face of printing type either by hand or as part of a machine press. (69)

ROMAN, the alphabets of capitals and lower-case letters usually designed upright, as against italic alphabets which are usually sloped. (36)

RULE, a type-high strip of brass or type-metal for printing straight, dotted or decorated lines of various widths. (32)

SANS SERIF, letters without SERIFS: A a, B b, C c. (91)

SERIF, finishing stroke at the end of a stem bar or terminal of normal letters. (91)

SET, the width of a type-body. (33)

SETTING, to pick up and arrange types for printing. Also COMPOSING. (13)

SET-OFF, the transference of ink from one printed sheet onto the back of another. (76)

SHANK, the body of a type, measured in points from back to front (=depth). (33)

SHOULDER, the non-printing area surrounding the face of a type. (33)

SIGNATURE, a section of a book made by folding a printed sheet so that the pages follow in correct order.

SIGNATURE MARK, a code printed on the first page of each signature.

SMALL CAPITALS, as here, cast on the same body as normal CAPITALS. (32)

SORT, any single type character. A special sort is a character not supplied in the normal fount. (31)

SPACES, pieces of type-metal varying in size and thickness and less than type-height, used for spacing letters and words. (34)

SPINE LABEL, a pasted label on the spine of a book usually giving title, author's and publisher's names. (82)

SUPERIOR, a special sort cast on the body so that it prints above the lower-case letters, m^2, m^3.

SWASH CHARACTERS, italic types with flourishes. (34)

TENON SAW, fine saw for cutting wooden furniture. (58)

TITLE-PAGE, one of the preliminary pages of a book on which one might expect to find the title, author's and publisher's names and sometimes further details concerning the contents of the book. (38)

TITLING FOUNT, a set of capital letters each cast to occupy the whole depth of the body.

TOGGLE, mechanical joint to transmit pressure at right angles (see diagram below). (22)

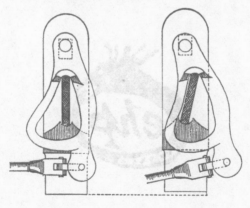

TYMPAN, the packing on the platen of a press, or the parchment-covered frames hinged at the bed of an Albion press. (22)

TYPE-HEIGHT (see HEIGHT-TO-PAPER).

UNDERLAY, part of the process of make-ready whereby packing is placed between the type and the bed of the press. (73)

UPPER-CASE, or capital letters, A B C D.

X-HEIGHT, the height of lower-case letters without extruders, as x m n u.

VERSO, the left-hand page, normally folioed with even numbers. The underside of a leaf. (38)

WATERMARK, a design made of wire and impressed into paper while it is being made. (86)

WOODCUT, a design cut in relief with a knife on the surface of a wood block or plank. (69)

WOOD ENGRAVING, a design in relief cut on the endgrain surface of wood with a graver – hence white line engraving. The techniques for a woodcut and a wood engraving are frequently mixed.

Joseph Low's Eden Hill Press mark as a tailpiece about to be enjoyed.

APPENDIX

The Miniature Folio of
Private Presses
1960

Note on the Folio

In 1959, four years after the first edition of *Printing for Pleasure* was published, I invited forty-four private presses to contribute 100 copies of a specific form of announcement about their work and their equipment. Only twenty-eight printers completed the project but of these most kept reasonably close to the given specifications. A portfolio containing one example from each of the presses was made and distributed in 1960 to the contributors, to a number of libraries and to distinguished persons associated with fine printing. Amongst the contributors was the Officina Bodoni (Dr Mardersteig was the only contributor who showed me a proof). In these final pages I have included the complete Miniature Press example (the published specimen shown in advance to all forty-four printers) and examples from six others.

THE

ESTABLISHED IN 1935

MINIATURE

OWNED BY JOHN RYDER

PRESS

RICHMOND, SURREY

ENGLAND

THE MINIATURE PRESS

4 Cambrian Road, Richmond, Surrey

GROUP III : EXPERIMENTAL

PRESS

Hand-operated flatbed (10 × 8)

TYPES

Albertus, Bell, Bembo, Castellar
Clarendon, Georgian open
Gresham, Grotesque 9
Fry's Ornamented

FLOWERS

A selection of types and 32 matrices
[see *A Suite of Fleurons*, 1956]

PAPER

A variety of samples
[see *Miniature Press Papers*, 1958]

ROMAN

Monotype Garamond 156 Italic

TITLING

alphabets in 14 point

FROM

The Stempel titling is Garamond 42 point

STEMPEL

Miniature Folio of

Private Presses

1960

GLI ULTIMI
DUE SONETTI

di

PETRARCA

SET IN DANTE TYPE FOR
MINIATURE FOLIO OF PRIVATE PRESSES
1960

From the press of Giovanni Mardersteig

This press was established
in December 1956 by
SUSAN MAHON
and its offices may
be found in
LONDON
South of the Thames

From

Philobiblon

by

RICHARD DE BURY

The Tuinwijkpress
Haarlem

From the press of S. L. Hartz

A B C
D E F G H I
K L M N
O P Q *Hendrik van den Keere* R
S T V X
Y Z

Two pages from the press of Mike Parker (and associates)

THE BARBER HILL PRESS

Green River Road, Colrain, Mass.

APOLOGIA
&
DETAILS

*A Contribution to
the Miniature Folio
of Private Presses*

1960

From the press of F. E. Pardoe

*From the press of Willis Tompkins, showing some of
his wood engravings.*